A Commentary on
The Sonnets of G.M. Hopkins

A
Commentary
on the
Sonnets
of
G.M. Hopkins

Peter Milward, S.J.

Loyola University Press
Chicago 60657

Loyola University Press
3441 North Ashland Avenue
Chicago, Illinois 60657

This book was originally published by the
Hokuseido Press, Tokyo, Japan, and is here
reprinted with permission by Loyola
University Press, Chicago.

Library of Congress Cataloging in Publication Data
Milward, Peter.
    A commentary on the sonnets of G.M. Hopkins.

    Reprint, Originally published: Tokyo: Hokuseido
Press, c1969.
    1. Hopkins, Gerard Manley, 1844-1889—Criticism
and interpretation. 2. Sonnets, English—History and
criticism. I. Title.
PR4803.H44Z718 1985   821'.8   85-5200
ISBN 0-8294-0494-5

"We should explain things, plainly state them, clear them up, explain them; explanation—except personal—is always pure good; without explanation people go on misunderstanding; being once explained they thenceforward understand things; therefore always explain."

(Hopkins to Bridges, May 25, 1888)

CONTENTS

viii

Preface

The present volume is designed as a companion or sequel to my previous *Commentary on G.M. Hopkins' The Wreck of the Deutschland* (Hokuseido, Tokyo, 1968). In that work I devoted my attention to the task of elucidating the first major poem of Hopkins after his long period of "elected silence"—a poem which was described by his friend, Robert Bridges, as "a great dragon folded in the gate to forbid all entrance". Here I turn to the series of shorter poems, mostly in the sonnet form, which followed this eloquent breach of poetic silence at irregular intervals from 1877 till the poet's death in 1889. It is astonishing—yet only to be expected of the poet of *The Wreck of the Deutschland*—how much thought and association is compressed within the narrow limits of the sonnet form; and, more than any other poetry of its kind, it seems to call for detailed commentary and elucidation.

With regard to their form, these sonnets of Hopkins may be seen as the culmination of a rich poetic tradition, which was introduced into England from Italy about the time of the Elizabethan Renaissance. The sonnet was then regarded as a form of love poetry; and almost every major poet of the age produced not just one or two, but a whole series of sonnets in honour of some real or imagined "beloved". In the hands of Shakespeare, the form became a medium for profound reflections on human life and death, on time and immortality, as seen through the experience of love. A religious tendency, already implicit in many sonnets of Sidney, Spenser and Shakespeare, was further developed in Donne's *Holy Sonnets*, from which the original motive of love entirely disappeared. In the subsequent sonnets of Milton, the religious aspect was replaced by one that is more personal and autobiographical.

The combined influence of Shakespeare and Milton is particularly evident in the romantic sonnets of Wordsworth and Keats; while in those of Wordsworth there is an additional element of natural description. All these varied elements, or aspects, of the sonnet tradition are, as it were, fused in a new synthesis in Hopkins' sonnets, which are at once metaphysical and religious, personal and descriptive. The only element which is—for obvious reasons—unrepresented is the original one of romantic love.

At the same time, these sonnets show a considerable departure from the previous tradition. As in *The Wreck of the Deutschland*, the poet here twists the English vocabulary and grammar—to an extent that might have horrified Milton himself—so as to recapture in words his vivid perception of the "this-ness" of things. The intensity of his poetic feeling is likewise reflected in his original use of "sprung rhythm", which depends for effect not on the regular alternation of stressed and unstressed syllables (as is usual in English verse), but on the regular number of stressed syllables in each line. With this emphasis on metrical stress, and with an abundant recourse to alliteration, Hopkins looks back through the imported sonnet tradition to the native genius of the English language as expressed in Old English poetry up to Langland's *Piers Plowman*. He also rejoins the other tradition of the "poetry of meditation", thereby associating himself with his fellow Jesuit poet of the Elizabethan Age, Robert Southwell. It is partly this tradition which is behind the clear distinction in his sonnets between the octet, describing some experience, and the sestet, drawing a religious conclusion.

Within this original sonnet form, there are further original variations, in which the poet seems to be exploring the utmost possibilities of the form. On the one hand, there is the "curtal" (or curtailed) form of sonnet, as represented in the two examples of *Pied Beauty* and *Peace*, where the normal division of octet and sestet is replaced by that of sestet and quatrain followed by a short line. Thus, instead of the traditional 14 lines, there are only 11, with a metrical scheme of abc abc—dbc dc. There are also several sonnets, including the "curtal" sonnet *Peace*, in which the usual five-stressed line is replaced throughout by a six-stressed "alexandrine". On the other hand, the sonnet form is prolonged in a variety of ways: with eight stresses per line, as in *Spelt from Sibyl's Leaves* (which the poet called "the longest sonnet ever made"); with "burden lines", as in *Harry Ploughman*; and with "codas" attached to 14 five-stressed lines, as in *Tom's Garland*, or to 14 alexandrines, as in *That Nature is a Heraclitean Fire*.

With regard to their content, the sonnets may be seen as revolving round two opposite poles of light and darkness. On the one hand, there are the "bright" sonnets, composed for the most part at St. Beuno's College in North Wales during 1877, in the aftermath of *The Wreck of the Deutschland*. They celebrate the mysterious presence of God within "the world's splendour and wonder" (WD 5), which evokes an enthusiastic response in the heart of the poet. They continue, with diminishing frequency, during his sojourn at Oxford in 1879, at Liverpool in 1880–1, and at Stonyhurst in 1882. But in a letter from Stonyhurst, addressed to Bridges, and dated July 26, 1883, the poet complains of declining health which affects his inspiration:

"I shall be sorry to leave Stonyhurst; but go or stay, there is no likelihood of my ever doing anything to last. And I do not know how it is, I have no disease, but I am always tired, always jaded, though work is not heavy, and the impulse to do anything fails me or has in it no continuance." (LB 183)

On the other hand, there are the "dark" sonnets, composed after his settling in Dublin as a professor at the university there, most of them during the summer of 1885. In them he feels only the absence of God, as he turns his thoughts increasingly upon his sick self. Yet in them he still looks insistently towards a comfort that gradually dawns on his mind through faith and patience—a comfort that is celebrated in his final poem of major proportions, *That Nature is a Heraclitean Fire and of the Comfort of the Resurrection.*

In the present volume, I have accordingly arranged the sonnets in their chronological sequence round these two poles of light and darkness, with a middle section for the intervening sonnets, composed at Oxford and Stonyhurst. which show more of light than of darkness. For reasons of space, I have decided to limit myself to the simpler form of sonnets, avoiding the more elaborate experiments that venture beyond the 14-line limit. I have printed the sonnets in the same typographical form as they appear in the recent fourth edition of the *Poems*, edited by W.H. Gardner and N.H. Mackenzie (Oxford University Press, 1967). But to facilitate their reading aloud, I have decided to add stress-marks, following the poet's own indications wherever possible, and otherwise relying on my private judgment. In my commentary on each poem, I have tried to be faithful to the thought of the poet, interpreting his words in the light of their context, of his other writings, and of his intellectual background as a Jesuit priest of the Victorian era. There remain many aspects of his poems, such as their sound effects. on which I have not touched; since it has been my chief aim to elucidate the difficulties of meaning and grammatical construction which often prevent the reader from deriving the fullest enjoyment from the poems. Once the intellectual obstacles are overcome, the poetic genius of Hopkins shines out—I am convinced—in all its brilliance, "as skies betweenpie mountains" (*My own heart*).

Sophia University,
Tokyo.   Peter Milward, S. J.

NOTE

The following abbreviations are used in the text:—

WD: *The Wreck of the Deutschland*

JP: *The Journals and Papers of Gerard Manley Hopkins* (ed. Humphrey House, Oxford University Press, 1959)

LB: *The Letters of Gerard Manley Hopkins to Robert Bridges* (ed. Claude Colleer Abbott, Oxford University Press, 1935)

LD: *The Correspondence of Gerard Manley Hopkins and Richard Watson Dixon* (ed. Claude Colleer Abbott, Oxford University Press, 1935)

FL: *Further Letters of Gerard Manley Hopkins* (ed. Claude Colleer Abbott, Oxford University Press, 1938; enlarged edition, 1956)

SD: *The Sermons and Devotional Writings of Gerard Manley Hopkins* (ed. Christopher Devlin, Oxford University Press, 1959)

I.

St. Beuno's, 1877

1.

God's Grandeur

God's Grandeur

THE wórld is chárged wíth the grándeur of Gód.
  It will fláme oút, like shíning from shóok fóil;
  It gáthers to a gréatness, líke the óoze of óil
Crushed. Whý do mén then nów not réck his ród?
Génerátions have tród, have tród, have tród;   5
  And áll is séared with tráde; bleared, sméared
      with tóil;
  And wéars man's smúdge and sháres man's sméll:
      the sóil
Is báre now, nór can fóot féel, being shód.

And for áll thís, náture is néver spént;
  There líves the déarest fréshness déep down thíngs; 10
And thóugh the lást lights óff the bláck West wént
  Oh, mórning, át the brówn brink eástward, spríngs—
Becáuse the Hóly Ghóst óver the bént
  World bróods with wárm breast ánd with áh!
      bright wíngs.

Commentary: The earliest version of the poem is dated Feb. 23, 1877. It is discussed by the poet in a letter to Bridges for Jan. 4, 1883.

1 The main theme of the sonnet is stated from the outset, that the world is charged with God's grandeur, as with electricity. Cf. Ps. lxxi. 19: "The whole earth shall be filled with his majesty." This idea represents the climax of the *Spiritual Exercises* of St. Ignatius in the Contemplation for Obtaining Love. On the final point of this Contemplation Hopkins himself comments:
"All things therefore are charged with love, are charged with God and if we know how to touch them give off sparks and take fire, yield drops and flow, ring and tell of him." (SD 195)

2 The presence of God is manifested in one of two ways. At times, it flames out with sudden brilliance, as when silver foil is shaken and gives out glints of light. Hopkins himself defines foil "in its sense of leaf or tinsel", and adds:
"Shaken goldfoil gives off broad glares like sheet lightning and also, and this is true of nothing else, owing to its zigzag dints and creasings and network of small many cornered facets, a sort of fork lightning too." (LB 169)

3 At other times, its greatness becomes apparent over a period of time, as when the oil crushed from an olive slowly oozes out and gathers into a thick pool. These two ways are elsewhere illustrated in the lives of St. Paul—"as once at a crash Paul"—and of St. Augustine—"or as Austin, a lingering-out sweet skill" (WD 10).

4 It is the second way which here arrests the poet's attention. The word "crushed", placed impressively at the head of the fourth line, makes him reflect on human misery, as being at once the consequence of sin and a means of atonement. It is the divine rod that both smites and heals. He therefore demands why men no longer heed this rod, or recognize the just punishments of God.

5   His answer is that men are inured to misery and have
    come to regard it with fatalistic eyes. Their senses
    have grown dull both to pain and to its cause. Life
    has come to seem a monotonous treadmill, with the
    weary routine of day following day from one gener-
    ation to another—as in Macbeth's "Tomorrow and
    tomorrow and tomorrow" (v. 5).

6   The love of money has left its black mark on every-
    thing, defacing the freshness of nature with selfish
    toil. The outcome is vividly expressed by the succes-
    sion of onomatopoeic words, "seared...bleared,
    smeared"—the first implying deep burning on the
    skin, the second, confused filming over the eyes, and
    the third, a muddy covering over the body.

7   The dirt and smell of human selfishness has now been
    communicated to the whole world of nature.

8   The earth is now bare and shorn of living beauty, as
    in winter. Man, too, remains insensitive no less to
    the present bareness than to the past beauty; even
    as his feet, being shod with shoes, are separated no
    less from the hardness than from the softness of the
    earth.

9   Such considerations would seem to encourage pessi-
    mism. But the poet shows how religious faith rises
    above this pessimism to an ultimate optimism, looking
    from darkness to light, from night to day, from winter
    to spring. In spite of all this wanton destruction of
    nature, her secret resources are never exhausted.

10 In the depths of her being there is a never-failing
    source of freshness, with which she is renewed each
    spring-time. This is what Hopkins elsewhere describes
    as "a strain of the earth's sweet being in the begin-
    ning in Eden garden" (*Spring*), or "that cheer and
    charm of earth's past prime" (*The Sea and the
    Skylark*).

11 He compares his weariness in the industrial age to
    the blackness of night, as in *Spelt from Sibyl's Leaves*,

after the twilight of sunset has faded in the west. Cf. Shakespeare's *Sonnet* lxxiii.

12 But he now looks with eager hope to a renewal of life, which he compares to the sunrise or "dayspring" rising above the eastern horizon. The "brown brink" refers rather to the brightness, or burnished appearance, of the sunrise than to the precise colour of the clouds—according to the meaning of OE "brun."

13 The religious grounds of his hope are stated in the final couplet, which reads like one line. It is the continued brooding of the Holy Ghost over the "bent world," as over the original waters of creation (*Genesis* i. 2), which brings forth renewed life from generation to generation. Here the adjective "bent" contains a significant ambiguity between the sense of crooked or evil, due to the selfish desire of material gain, and that of the object of "bending" compassion, through which the pure love of goodness restores life to the world.

14 The final line emphasizes the motherly love of God, comparing his care to that of a mother bird brooding over the eggs in her nest. Her "warm breast" evokes the thought of his love, and her "bright wings", the light of his salvation.

2.

The Starlight Night

The Starlight Night

LÓOK at the stárs! lóok, look úp at the skíes!
  O lóok at áll the fíre-folk sítting in the áir!
  The bríght bóroughs, the círcle-cítadels thére!
Dówn in dim wóods the díamond délves! the
    elves'-éyes!
The gréy lawns cóld where góld, where quíckgold líes!   5
  Wínd-beat whítebeam! aíry abeles sét on a fláre!
  Fláke-doves sent flóating fórth at a fármyard scáre!
Áh well! it is áll a púrchase, áll is a príze.

Búy then! bíd then!—Whát?—Prayer, pátience,
    alms, vóws.
Look, lóok: a Máy-mess, líke on órchard bóughs!   10
  Look! Márch-bloom, líke on méaled-with-yéllow
    sállows!
Thése are indéed the bárn; withíndoors hóuse
The shócks. This píece-bright páling shúts the spoúse
  Christ hóme, Chríst and his móther and áll his
    hállows.

Commentary: The poem is dated Feb. 24, 1877. It recalls an experience of the poet which is recorded in his journal for Aug. 17, 1874:

> "As we drove home the stars came out thick: I leant back to look at them and my heart opening more than usual praised Our Lord to whom and in whom all that beauty comes home." (JP 254)

1 Here the poet expresses enthusiastic delight in the beauty of a night sky, as in WD 5: "I kiss my hand to the stars, lovely-asunder starlight." With impulsive eagerness he points up at the stars, repeating the same exclamation, "Look!"

2 In a childish rapture he views the stars as people sitting in the sky. Similarly, in *Spelt from Sibyl's Leaves*, he speaks of "fire-featuring heaven" with "her earliest stars, earl-stars, stars principal".

3 He then goes on to present them not as individual persons, but as walled cities or "boroughs" each defended by a citadel, as in mediaeval times.

4 With the preposition "down" he apparently deflects his attention from heaven to earth, where the woods are dim in the starlight. Hidden in their "delves" or secret recesses, the mines dug by dwarfs, are dewy diamonds, sparkling like the eyes of the elves who have found them. Or it may be that the poet is speaking of heaven in terms of earth.

5 Beneath the cold grey open spaces, or "lawns", is likewise hidden fairy gold, which is liquid like quicksilver. Literally, "quickgold" means living gold.

6 Within the woods he discerns the sturdy white-beam with its silver foliage blown by the wind, and the lofty abele, or white poplar, with the stars appearing among the branches so that they seem to be "set on a flare".

7 The movement of their silvery leaves in the wind reminds him of doves flying up from the dovecote in

the farmyard on the occasion of a sudden alarm. The association of "flake" with "doves" also contains the suggestion of falling snow.

8 Reflecting on all this unearthly beauty, he becomes calmer, and changes his "O!" to an "Ah!" After all, it is not a free gift to the human spectator. It has to be bought as a purchase, to be won as a prize; or else it simply vanishes. Hopkins is here thinking of the lines from Herbert's *Church-Porch* (st. 29):

> "Take stars for money; stars not to be told
> By any art, but to be purchased."

9 He therefore draws the practical conclusion: it must all be bought, bid for. But in terms of what currency? The only currency valid for purchasing such beauty is that of religious devotion: prayer, fasting and almsdeeds (the three traditional works of religion), together with the three religious vows of poverty, chastity and obedience.

10 But he cannot long remain calm in his present state of excitement. He again points up at the stars, as they appear among the boughs of the trees, like May-blossom in the orchard, with its red and white flowers —"when drop-of-blood-and-foam-dapple bloom lights the orchard-apple" (*The May Magnificat*).

11 He is also reminded of the glossy catkins in March, as they hang down from the sallows (a kind of willow-tree) with yellow meal or dust on their furry coats.

12 Yet amid his excitement he recognizes that all this beauty is but the outside of the "barn" of heaven, concealing "withindoors" an even more wonderful reality.

13 This reality is "the shocks", or sheaves of good grain, which symbolize the just in Christ's parable of the harvest (*Matthew* xiii. 30). Similarly, the poet asks in WD 31: "Is the shipwrack then a harvest, does tempest carry the grain for thee?" What he sees with his eyes, "what by your measure is the heaven

of desire" (WD 26), is but a fence or "paling" whose every stake is bright with stars.

14 Within he finds himself "home at heart" (*To what serves Mortal Beauty*) with Christ, who is traditionally called the "spouse" or bridegroom of the Church, according to St. John's *Apocalypse*. With Christ he finds Mary his mother and all his saints, or "hallows" as they are called in mediaeval English.

N.B. The movement of thought in the octet seems to follow not only a natural association of images, but also an alphabetical order of alliteration: a) *a*ll, *a*ir; b) *b*right *b*oroughs; c) *c*ircle-*c*itadels; d) *d*own, *d*im, *d*iamond *d*elves; e) *e*lves'-*e*yes. There follows an inversion between g) *g*rey, *g*old, quick*g*old, and f) *f*lare, *f*lake, *f*loating *f*orth, *f*armyard. Such *tours de force* are not uncommon in Hopkins' poems.

3.

Spring

Spring

NÓTHING ís so béautifúl as Spríng—
  When wéeds, in whéels, shoot lóng and lóvely
    and lúsh;
  Thrúsh's éggs look líttle low héavens, and thrúsh
Through the échoing tímber dóes so rínse and wríng
The éar, it stríkes like líghtnings to héar him síng;   5
  The glássy péartree léaves and blóoms, they brúsh
  The descénding blúe; that blúe is áll in a rúsh
With ríchness; the rácing lambs tóo have fáir their
    flíng.

Whát is áll this júice and áll this jóy?
  A stráin of the éarth's sweet béing ín the begínning   10
In Éden gárden.—Háve, gét, before it clóy,

  Before it clóud, Chríst, lórd, and sóur with sínning,
Ínnocent mínd and Máyday in gírl and bóy,
  Most, Ó maid's chíld, thy chóice and wórthy the
    wínning.

Commentary: The poem is dated May, 1877.

1 The poet begins this sonnet, as so often, with a general proposition, commending the beauty of Spring. His use of a capital letter for "Spring" seems to imply personification.

2 He proceeds to describe the beauty of Spring with reference to a particular country scene: of a hedgerow by the roadside, with a meadow beyond. His attention is first engaged by the "weeds" or wild flowers growing at his feet. He notes how they send forth long shoots, "lovely and lush" in their freshness and rich luxuriance. "In wheels" means, metaphorically, turning over and over, with graceful curves, as their shoots push out farther and farther.

3 Raising his eyes from the ground, he further notices a thrush's nest, with its blue eggs mottled with black spots. They look to him like "little low heavens" studded with stars. Similarly, in *The May Magnificat*, he contemplates the "throstle above her nested/ Cluster of bugle blue eggs".

4 Next, he listens to the song of the thrush echoing through the timber of the hedgerow, like a kind of sounding-board, and as it were cleansing his ear with its liquid purity. In "rinse and wring" there is an idea of the pain that purifies—as in WD 9: "Wring thy rebel," and in the sonnet *No worst*: "More pangs will . . . wilder wring . . . wince and sing." There is also an intentional association of sound with "ring".

5 He compares the waves of sound striking his ear to the effect of lightning on his eye—like the "flashing out" of *God's Grandeur*. The plural form is used to indicate the succession of sounds, as in the "profuse strains of unpremeditated art" of Shelley's *Skylark*.

6 With his eyes he follows the sound to the branches of a peartree, which stand out vividly against the blue sky. Its leaves and blossoms seem bright as

glass in the sunshine, and almost touching the blue of the sky.

7 The blue itself seems to be descending from heaven to earth "in a rush" with the richness of its new life. The same idea is expressed in WD 26: "Blue-beating" (of the heavens in May), and in *The Blessed Virgin compared to the Air we Breathe*: "Look overhead/ How air is azured/...do but stand/ Where you can lift your hand/ Skywards: rich, rich it laps/ Round the four fingergaps."

8 The new life is particularly manifested by the young lambs whom he notices frisking about in the meadow beyond. As they race with each other, they seem to fling themselves from the earth in new-found delight. This very scene is described in his journal for Apr. 16, 1871: "The young lambs...toss and toss; it is as if it were the earth that flung them, not themselves." (JP 206) The predicative use of "fair" recalls its similar use in *Henry Purcell*: "Have fair fallen, O fair, fair have fallen..."

9 The poet now pauses to reflect on this spring scene in a spirit of meditation and prayer. He asks himself what it all means, all this sap of life flowing through nature and filling with joy both plant and tree, bird and beast.

10 He finds his answer, as in *God's Grandeur*, in "the dearest freshness deep down things", the ever recurring strain of sweetness that continues to flow through the earth from the garden of Eden. For it is in the spring that "earth's past prime" is renewed from year to year, in spite of man's sin.

11 On the other hand, this freshness is always fading away, in man no less than in nature. This thought prompts him to turn to Christ with the prayer, "Sume et suscipe"—"Take and receive"—as proposed by St. Ignatius in the Contemplation for Obtaining Love.

12 He turns to Christ as "lord", as so often in WD and

in *The Windhover*; since he alone can preserve the purity and innocence of man, which, without him, all too soon clouds over like an April day, or (to vary the metaphor) falls into excess, whether of sweetness or of sourness, by sin.

13 The special object of his concern is the innocent mind of youth, which he finds symbolized in the freshness of "Mayday".

14 Such virginal innocence is particularly prized by Christ, who is himself the child of Mary the Virgin—as the poet also remarks in WD 30: "Jesu, maid's son." Here he may well have been thinking of Robert Southwell's poem, *A Child my Choice*. Like the beauty of *The Starlight Night*, such purity is not merely a gift, but "it is all a purchase, all is a prize"—and one well "worthy the winning".

N.B. The title of the sonnet seems to be echoed throughout by means of the many rhyming words in -ing, from "Nothing" to "winning". The rhymes in between vary the significance of sound: with -ush in the octet, expressing the sensuous richness of the season (as also in WD 8), and -oy in the sestet, expressing the open movement of spiritual joy reaching up from earth to heaven.

4.

In the Valley of the Elwyn

In the Valley of the Elwyn

Í REMÉMBER a hóuse where áll were góod
    To mé, God knóws, desérving nó such thíng:
    Cómforting sméll bréathed at very éntering,
Fetched frésh, as Í suppóse, off sóme sweet wóod.
That córdial áir made thóse kind péople a hóod   5
    All óver, as a bévy of éggs the móthering wíng
    Will, or míld níghts the néw morsels of Spríng:
Why, it séemed of cóurse; séemed of ríght it shóuld.

Lovely the wóods, wáters, méadows, cómbes, váles,
All the áir things wéar that búild this wórld of Wáles; 10
    Ónly the ínmate dóes not córrespónd:

God, lóver of sóuls, swáying consíderate scáles,
Compléte thy créature déar O whére it fáils,
    Being míghty a máster, béing a fáther and fónd.

Commentary: The poem is dated "May 23, 1877". Its title points to the valley of the Elwy, which merges with the larger vale of Clwyd near St. Asaph. But the octet refers to a house in Kent, as Hopkins explains in a letter to Bridges dated April 8, 1879:

> "The kind people of the sonnet were the Watsons of Shooter's Hill, nothing to do with the Elwy. The facts were as stated. You misunderstand the thought, which is very far fetched. The frame of the sonnet is a rule of three sum *wrong*, thus: As the sweet smell to those kind people so the Welsh landscape is NOT to the Welsh; and then the author and principle of all four terms is asked to bring the sum right." (LB 76–7)

1 The poet begins by recalling the kindness he received from the Watsons of Shooter's Hill, in a line reminiscent of Thomas Hood's well-known poem:
> "I remember, I remember
> The house where I was born,"

2 He appreciates this kindness all the more in contrast to his own feeling of unworthiness in the sight of God.

3 Corresponding to this kindness, he notes the characteristic fragrance perceptible at the very entrance to the house and symbolic of the welcome accorded there to visitors.

4 The fragrance comes from a vase of flowers, newly plucked from a nearby wood and placed on a table by the hall-door. Here the poet is perhaps thinking of Wordsworth's line in *The Tables Turned*: "One impulse from a vernal wood."

5 Such an atmosphere is "cordial", both in the literal sense of health-giving, like a tonic, and in the metaphorical sense of welcoming. It covers these people like a hood all over.

6 In this connection, the poet instinctively recalls the image of a mother bird making a hood over her eggs

with her outstretched wings—like the "star-eyed strawberry-breasted/ Throstle above her nested/ Cluster of bugle blue eggs thin" in *The May Magnificat.* The collective word "bevy" is properly applied to a flock of birds; but Hopkins extends its use to the eggs.

7   Similarly, mild nights in spring make a hood over the "new morsels", that is, over the newly emerging "leaves and blooms" mentioned in *Spring*. In these two lines the grammatical structure is rather elliptical: corresponding to "that cordial air" are "the mothering wing" and "mild nights", while corresponding to "those kind people" are "a bevy of eggs" and "the new morsels of Spring". "Will" has the sense of "is wont to (make a hood all over)", and it is implied in the further example.

8   Finally, as though brushing aside the question "Why?", he adds that this phenomenon was but natural ("of course") and fitting ("of right"). The "of" before "right" sounds rather odd; but it harmonizes with "of course", and corresponds to the Latin "de iure". Cf. Hopkins' use of an extra "a" in WD 4: "I steady as a water in a well, to a poise, to a pane," and an extra "the" in WD 16: "dandled the to and fro."

9   He then goes on to draw the contrast between this house in Kent and the "world of Wales". There is, indeed, a parallel in the beauty of natural scenery. The "combes" mentioned may refer to deep wooded valleys among the hills, as they are called in Devonshire, or perhaps to the hills themselves by association with the name of a hill near St. Beuno's College, Cwm.

10   The "cordial air" spoken of above is matched by "all the air" which seems to clothe everything that makes Wales what it is. The poet's love of the Welsh countryside is likewise expressed in WD 24: "Away in the loveable west,/ On a pastoral forehead of Wales."

11   But the painful contrast comes when he turns to the people who live there. They, the inhabitants or

"inmates", do not correspond to the air that surrounds them, like those mentioned in *The Sea and the Skylark* as dwelling in the "shallow and frail town" of Rhyl.

12 He therefore turns in supplication to God the Father, as "lover of souls", who is not only just, "swaying" the scales of reward and punishment, but also merciful and "considerate" towards human weakness. The mention of "scales" here recalls WD 21: "Thy unchancelling poising palms were weighing the worth."

13 He asks God to supply for the deficiencies of man, who is his dear creature — albeit "dear and dogged", as he calls man in the companion poem of *Ribblesdale*. The addition of "O" in the middle of the line is expressive of his intense desire.

14 He expects God to bring about man's perfection, not merely by the exercise of power or "mastery", but chiefly by the manifestation of fatherly love and "mercy". These are the two attributes of God on which he insists in WD, especially in st. 9–10. "A father and fond" echoes WD 9: "Father and fondler of heart thou hast wrung." The adjectives "mighty" and "fond" are placed in the predicative position for emphasis. The rhyme of "fond" with "correspond" indicates the way by which the correspondence is to be achieved.

5.

The Sea and the Skylark

The Sea and the Skylark

ON éar and éar two nóises too óld to énd
  Trench—ríght, the tíde that rámps agaínst the
      shóre;
  With a flóod or a fáll, low lúll-off or áll róar,
Frequénting thére while móon shall wéar and wénd.

Léft hand, off lánd, I héar the lárk ascénd,   5
  His rásh-fresh re-wínded néw-skéinèd scóre
  In crísps of cúrl off wíld winch whírl, and póur
And pélt músic, till nóne's to spíll nor spénd.

How thése two sháme this shállow and fráil tówn!
  How ríng right óut our sórdid túrbid tíme,   10
Being púre! Wé, life's príde and cáred-for crówn,

    Have lóst that chéer and chárm of eárth's past
        príme:
  Our máke and máking bréak, are bréaking, dówn
    To mán's last dúst, drain fást towards mán's
        first slíme.

Commentary: The poem is dated "Rhyl, May 1877", a seaside town about 8 miles from St. Beuno's College. It was originally entitled "Walking by the Sea". Hopkins gives a detailed explanation of this poem, in its first version, to his friend Bridges in a letter dated Nov. 26, 1882. He remarks, somewhat apologetically:

> "The sonnet you ask about is the greatest offender in its way that you could have found. It was written in my Welsh days, in my salad days, when I was fascinated with *cynghanedd* or consonant chime." (LB 163)

1 The poet begins by describing two natural noises which come to "ear and ear" from opposite directions, as he is walking along the sea-shore. They are at once as old and as fresh as the world of nature, to which they belong, and therefore "too old to end".

2 Their effect on his senses is vividly expressed by the verb "trench", which adds to the meaning of "impress" the further associations with "drench" (the sea on the sand) and "crunch" (the sound of falling waves). On the right hand, he notes the noise of the tide regularly breaking against the shore. The shore itself he conceives, as in WD 1 and 32, as a rampart against the continual onslaught of the waters, which "ramp" or "romp" about like a sportive wild animal (cf. also "the sea-romp" in WD 17).

3 With each wave the water floods out over the shore and then recedes; with a corresponding alternation in sound between the lull after the breaking of the wave and the all-out roar of the next. This contrast between flood and fall also appears in WD 32, where God is described as "master of the tides,/ Of the Yore-flood, of the year's fall". "Lull-off" is a combination of lull and leave off, as in the sonnet *No worst*: "Then lull, then leave off."

4 This alternating noise continues to "frequent" the shore so long as the moon, which rules the tides,

continues to "wear", or wane, and "wend", or wax,
that is, to decrease or increase.

5 On the left hand, where the land comes down to the
sea, he hears the other noise of a skylark singing as
he flies up into the sky—"off", that is, above the land.

6 His song, ever the same, seems to follow a musical
"score", which is compared to a "skein" of wool
that is successively unwound as he sings in the sky
and re-wound on his return to earth; so that each
song is as fresh as the one before. In his letter to
Bridges, Hopkins explains "rash-fresh" as

"a headlong and exciting new snatch of singing,
resumption by the lark of his song, which by turns
he gives over and takes up again all day long, and
this goes on, the sonnet says, through all time without ever losing its first freshness, being a thing
both new and old." (LB 164)

He goes on to explain "new-skeined score" as referring to

"the lark's song, which from his height gives the
impression (not to me only) of something falling to
the earth and not vertically quite but tricklingly or
wavingly, something as a skein of silk ribbed by
having been tightly wound on a narrow card or a
notched holder or as fishing tackle or twine unwinding from a reel or winch: the laps or folds are
the notes or short measures and bars of them. The
same is called a score in the musical sense of score
and this score is 'writ upon a liquid sky trembling
to welcome it', only not horizontally." (ibid.)

7 This score the lark seems to whirl off the winch of
his throat in a wild ecstasy, not in a smooth, even
flow, but as it were in crisp curls of melody—whose
every note is likened to a lock of fleece waving in the
air. The precise idea is again explained by Hopkins:

"The lark in wild glee races the reel round, pay-
ing or dealing out and down the turns of the skein
or coil right to the earth floor, the ground, where

it lies in a heap, as it were, or rather is all wound off on to another winch, reel, bobbin, or spool in Fancy's eye by the moment the bird touches earth and so is ready for a fresh unwinding at the next flight." (ibid.)

This favourite image recurs, in a rather different context, in *Spelt from Sibyl's Leaves*: "Let life, waned, ah let life wind/ Off her once skeined stained veined variety ׀ upon, all on two spools."

8 The lark seems to pour without effort, and yet to pelt with unceasing effort, his fresh song, till he has spilt and spent all and there is nothing left. He thus embodies the poet's ideal of "selving" through stress of being, of dealing "out that being indoors each one dwells" (*As kingfishers catch fire*).

9 The poet proceeds, in the sestet, to contrast these two natural noises, whose purity makes them ever old and ever new, with the sordid sounds that reach his ears from the "shallow and frail town" of Rhyl—to the "shame" of the latter. This unflattering reference to the Welsh town of Rhyl is matched by his lament over "the inmate" of "this world of Wales" in his sonnet *In the Valley of the Elwy*.

10 Like the song of the thrush in *Spring*, these noises "rinse and wring the ear" by their liquid purity. They "ring out", like the "wild bells" of Tennyson's *In Memoriam* cvi, "to the wild sky" far above the turbid atmosphere of the town with its dirty rows of houses.

11 They put to shame not merely the houses, but their human inhabitants. Ideally, we are the lords of creation, the "pride" and "crown" of the natural world, "her bonniest, dearest to her, her clearest-selved spark" (*That Nature is a Heraclitean Fire*).

12 But now through sin, and in particular that selfishness which marks the industrial age, we have lost the joy

of "the earth's sweet being in the beginning in Eden garden" (*Spring*), when all things were in their prime.

13 Now our nature and natural inclination, "our make and making"—the static and dynamic aspects of our human being—are in process of decay and dissolution. The sense is here clearly echoed in the sound: with the contrast between "make" and "break", and between the positive and progressive forms of each verb. It is the same sense as in WD 4: "Mined with a motion."

14 The outcome of this process is the state of "dust" which awaits man in death, and which recalls his original state of "slime" (cf. *Genesis* ii. 7 for "slime", and iii. 19 for "dust"). This idea is energetically stated in WD 11: "But we dream we are rooted in earth—Dust!" It also contains an echo of Macbeth's "Way to dusty death" (v. 5). In this pessimistic emphasis on our bodily nature, our end rejoins our beginning; and on this pessimistic note the poet, too, somewhat uncharacteristically ends his poem.

6.

The Windhover

The Windhover

To Christ our Lord

I CÁUGHT this mórning mórning's mínion, kíng-
  dom of dáylight's dáuphin, dapple-dáwn-drawn
    Fálcon, in his ríding
Of the rólling level úndernéath him steady áir,
    and stríding
Hígh there, how he rúng upon the réin of a wím-
    pling wíng
In his écstasy! then óff, óff fórth on swíng,   5
  As a skáte's heel sweeps smóoth on a bów-bend:
    the húrl and glíding
Rebúffed the bíg wínd. My héart in híding
Stírred for a bírd,—the achíeve of, the mástery of
    the thíng!

Brute béauty and válour and áct, oh, air, príde,
    plume, hére
  Búckle! AND the fíre that bréaks from thée then,   10
    a bíllion
Tímes told lóvelier, more dángerous, O mý chevalíer!

  No wónder of it: shéer plód makes plóugh down
    síllion
Shíne, and blúe-bleak émbers, áh my déar,
  Fall, gáll themsélves, and gásh góld-vermílion.

Commentary: The poem is dated "St. Beuno's, May 30, 1877". In a letter to Bridges, of June 22, 1879, Hopkins describes it as "the best thing I ever wrote". Its title, "The Windhover", is the popular name of the kestrel, or small kind of hawk, so called from its habit of hovering in the wind. There is an exhibit with this name in the Waterton collection of stuffed birds and beasts, now at Stonyhurst College, but in Hopkins' time at St. Beuno's. The sub-title, "To Christ our Lord", was added later to emphasize the religious significance of the poem as a whole.

1 The appropriate setting for this poem is the morning, when the poet caught sight of the bird which is "morning's minion" or darling.

2 He speaks of it not by the common names of hawk or kestrel, but by the more aristocratic French-derived name of "falcon", with a capital F as though to indicate a personal, and even divine, significance. He describes it, in terms of mediaeval chivalry and French royalty, as the "dauphin" or crown prince of the "kingdom of daylight". With a characteristically compound adjective, he presents it as drawn by the dappled dawn, in contrast with the "dappled-with-damson west" of WD 5.

3 Developing the metaphor of chivalry, he sees the bird as bestriding the air beneath him like a skilful horseman controlling his horse. The air is at once rolling and yet level and steady underneath him, as he rides high and erect in the saddle. In this picture Hopkins may be recalling the Dauphin's praise of his horse in Shakespeare's *Henry V* iii. 7: "When I bestride him I soar, I am a hawk: he trots the air."

4 The bird circles in the air, as though controlling its movement in the wind after the manner of a trainer "ringing on the rein" of a wild horse. It pivots round on the tip of its extended wing, which is described

as "wimpling"—that is, pleated and rippling like a nun's wimple in movement.

5 In this supreme moment of conflict with the force of the wind the bird feels ecstasy, before sweeping off in the direction of the wind as though on a swing. Cf. "the swing of the sea" in *Heaven-Haven*.

6 This movement also reminds the poet of a skilful skater, sweeping round smoothly "on a bow-bend", that is, while cutting a figure of eight on the ice. It combines "hurl", or strong self-propulsion, with "gliding", or full utilization of the wind's force. The conjunction of "sweep" and "hurl" recurs in WD 2: "The sweep and the hurl of thee", and 13: "Into the snows she sweeps, hurling the haven behind"; and again in the journal for Nov. 8, 1874: (starlings that) "sweep around in whirlwinds...all narrow black flakes hurling round". (JP 261)

7 The skill of the bird thus seems to "rebuff the big wind", as in a triumph of mind over matter. It is this which inwardly stirs the heart of the poet. "In hiding" may refer a) to the fact that he is watching the bird from some hidden place, or b) to the fact that the heart is itself hidden in its "bower of bone" (WD 17), or c) to the fact that he is leading a hidden, religious life at St. Beuno's far from the world where "honour is flashed off exploit" (*St. Alphonsus Rodriguez*).

8 His heart stirs with admiration for the bird—for its achievement in triumphing over the inanimate forces of nature. He even ascribes to the bird a "mastery" which elsewhere he ascribes to God. He can only speak of it as "the thing", which is at once a confession of the poverty of human language and a successful refurbishing of this word as the culmination of eight rhymes in -ing (alternating between stressed -ing and unstressed -iding).

9 In the sestet, he sums up the qualities of the bird

first with a series of abstract nouns—its beauty, courage, energy ("act" in the Aristotelian sense)—and then with a more concrete hendiadys of three—the proud air of its plumes. Here he combines the common idioms: to give oneself airs, to take pride in, and to plume oneself on something.

10 "Here" may refer to the bird, or to his "heart in hiding", or to the whole situation, according to the particular interpretation given to these three lines. "Buckle" may mean a) fasten together, like a belt (here used in an intransitive sense), or b) crumple up, hence bow down, surrender, as in the phrase "buckle under". The tense of the verb may, further, be either indicative or (as seems implied by the exclamation mark) imperative. Account has also to be taken of the capitalizing of AND, which is thus emphasized outside the metrical stress of the line. Finally, "thee" may refer either to the bird, or to himself, or else to Christ, according to the meaning assigned to "my chevalier". Amid all these possibilities, it is not perhaps necessary to make an exclusive choice, considering Hopkins' deliberate use of ambiguity in his poems. But in so far as he generally turns in the sestet to reflect on himself, it is more likely that "here" has its primary reference to his "heart in hiding". "Buckle" may well include both meanings, of coming together and buckling under, with respect "to Christ our Lord". The "oh" and the following exclamation mark point to the imperative mood; but the whole construction is perhaps conditional in effect, as in the pattern: "Do this, and you will . . ." for "If you do this, you will . . ."—which explains the capitalization of AND. In this case, "thee" would also refer to his "heart in hiding", which he conceives as a "chevalier" or knight, according to St. Ignatius' Meditation on the Kingdom in *The Spiritual Exercises*. That is to say, it is precisely by recollecting all his mental powers and submitting them to Christ as King, that the "fire" of divine beauty and love breaks from him—even as

"the grandeur of God" flashes out "like shining from shook foil". At the same time, it is a fire which breaks from Christ, the true Dauphin, who is figured in the falcon; for then is man a true "chevalier" when he is one with Christ.

11 This spiritual fire is "a billion times told lovelier" in him than the "brute beauty" of the bird in its ecstatic flight, and yet "more dangerous" as making him a more effective warrior in the service of Christ. "Nothing venture, nothing have" is no less true of spiritual than of material exploits.

12 To confirm his assertion, and to lessen the "wonder" at "a billion times", the poet goes on to cite two examples taken from common experience. First, he notes how the mere plodding of a ploughman as he pushes his plough down the "sillion" or furrow (cf. French "sillon") produces a brightness on his plough-share; as Virgil also notes in *Georgics* I 46: "Sulco attritus splendescere vomer." In the same way, fidelity in religious life, which is compared by Christ to taking up the plough (*Luke* ix. 62), produces a spiritual brightness in the soul. This is what Hopkins finds in Christ himself, in a sermon dated Nov. 23, 1879:
>"Poor was his station, laborious his life, bitter his ending: through poverty, through labour, through crucifixion his majesty of nature more shines." (SD 37)

13 Secondly, he speaks of the embers of a fire that appear to be dead, bleak in their faded blue colour, but then interrupts himself with the exclamation, "Ah my dear!" The significance is derived from Herbert's poem, *Love*, where the poet is speaking in his own name to Christ:
>"I the unkind, ungrateful? Ah, my dear,
>I cannot look on thee."

14 It is precisely when these embers, seemingly lifeless (like the poet's soul), fall and bruise themselves, that

they break open and reveal a hidden fire of "gold-vermilion". Similarly, it is through suffering and mortification for the sake of Christ in his outwardly "blue-bleak" religious life that Hopkins hopes, like the sisters in WD 23, "to bathe in his fall-gold mercies, to breathe in his all-fire glances".

N.B.   This sonnet is a particularly fine example of Hopkins' use of "sprung rhythm." The spacious feeling produced by the many unstressed syllables in the first four lines culminates in the concentrated cluster of stressed syllables in the fifth line, which expresses the bird's ecstasy. The rhymes of the octet have, as noted above, a ringing sound of triumph, with a contrast between the masculine ending of -ing and the feminine ending of -iding. The climax of the octet in "the thing" is clinched by the even more impressive climax of the sestet in "gold-vermilion".

7.

Pied Beauty

Pied Beauty

GLÓRY bé to Gód for dáppled thíngs—
　For skíes of cóuple-cólour as a bríndedców;
　　For róse-moles áll in stípple upon tróut that
　　　swím;
Fresh-fírecoal chéstnut-fálls; fínches' wíngs;
　Lándscape plótted and píeced—fold, fállow, and　5
　　plóugh.
　And áll trádes, their géar and táckle and trím.

Áll things cóunter, oríginal, spáre, stránge;
　Whatéver is fíckle, fréckled (whó knows hów?)
　　With swíft, slow; swéet, sóur; adázzle, dím;
He fáthers-fórth whose béauty is pást chánge:　10
　　　　　　Práise hím.

Commentary: The poem is dated "St. Beuno's, Tremeir-
chion. Summer 1877." It is described as a "curtal
sonnet," that is, a shortened form of sonnet, with only
10½ lines and an altered rhyme scheme.

1 From the glorification of God in dappled things to the
final exhortation to praise, the movement of this poem
takes place between the two mottoes of St. Ignatius:
"Ad majorem Dei gloriam" (To the greater glory of
God) and "Laus Deo semper" (Praise be to God always).
In Jesuit schools it is customary for pupils to write
the former motto, A.M.D.G., at the beginning of each
written exercise, and the latter motto, L.D.S., at the
end. Thus it seems that Hopkins is treating his poem
as an exercise in the Jesuit manner.

As in *God's Grandeur* and *Spring*, he opens with a
general statement of a thesis; but here he presents it
in the form of a prayer of adoration, as in WD 9:
"Be adored among men." The glory of God, which
he recognizes in WD 5 as present "under the world's
splendour and wonder", he finds above all in "dappled
things", as in "the dappled-with-damson west." He
delights in the "pied beauty" of nature—its dappled,
mottled, variegated appearance, which he proceeds to
illustrate with various examples.

2 Following the order of the days of creation in *Genesis*,
he first mentions "skies of couple-colour," as seen in
"pied and peeled May" when the heavens are "jay-
blue" (WD 26). Somewhat oddly, he compares them
to the hide of a "brinded" or brindled cow, on which
brown is mixed with streaks of another colour. (Perhaps he thinking of the cow in the nursery rhyme
that jumped over the moon.)

3 Then, looking down to the river, he notices the trout
swimming around with their rose-coloured markings
"all in stipple", that is, spotted with black.

4 On the earth he first draws attention to the windfalls
from chestnut trees. Having fallen on the ground,
they break open, revealing the reddish brown nut

within, as it were "fresh-firecoal"—like the embers in *The Windhover* that "fall, gall themselves and gash gold-vermilion". Similarly, in his journal for Sept. 17 1868 Hopkins speaks of "chestnuts as bright as coals or spots of vermilion".
Among the birds in the branches, he notes the varied colours in the wings of finches.

5 Then he turns to the works of men, first in agriculture and pastoral activity, as being closer to the life of nature. The countryside is, in consequence, divided into small plots or pieces, like the patchwork of a quilt—some fields being used as "folds" for sheep, others lying "fallow" for a time as meadowland, and yet others under "plough" for various kinds of crops.

6 He finally mentions different kinds of industry, with emphasis not on the searing effect of trade, as in *God's Grandeur*, but on the neat order of equipment, "gear and tackle and trim", which seems to have special reference to sailing vessels, perhaps of fishermen.

7 In the quatrain, as in the sestet of *The Windhover*, the poet proceeds to sum up the general qualities he appreciates in such "dappled things". He admires the juxtaposition of contrary things in a kind of counterpoint, their uniqueness and originality, their rarity that makes them precious, their oddness that makes each one stand out by itself from all the rest, "crying *What I do is me: for that I came*" (*As kingfishers catch fire*).

8 He likes their very fickleness (irregularity in duration), which makes them unpredictable like the English weather, and their freckled or speckled appearance (irregularity in pattern), while pausing to raise the deep metaphysical question: "Who knows how?"—as in the old riddle: "Why has a cow got four legs?"

9 "Freckled" is not an absolute quality here, but related to the contrasting pairs of "swift, slow," as in the

hare and the tortoise, "sweet, sour", as in the taste
of "a lush-kept plush-capped sloe" in WD 8, and
"adazzle, dim", as in WD 34: "Not a doomsday
dazzle in his coming nor dark as he came".

10 In conclusion, he states — what he has already implied
in the opening line — that all these things flow from
their source in the paternal being of him "whose
beauty is past change." With this simple statement
he touches on the theological problem which exercised
the mind of Duns Scotus — how the various attributes
in God can be really distinguished from one another
without prejudice to the simplicity of his divine being.
He is mainly inspired by the concluding point of St.
Ignatius' Contemplation for Obtaining Love at the end
of the *Spiritual Exercises*:

"How all good things and gifts descend from above,
as my poor power from the supreme and infinite
power above, and similarly, justice, goodness, pity,
mercy, etc., just as from the sun descend rays, from
the fountain waters, etc."

11 The whole poem leads up to the practical conclusion
in the final coda, "Praise him" — with an effect of
aposiopesis. It echoes Cardinal Newman's famous
hymn: "Praise to the holiest in the height."

8.

Hurrahing in Harvest

Hurrahing in Harvest

SUMMER énds now; now, bárbarous in béauty, the
    stóoks ríse
Aróund; up abóve, what wínd-walks! what lóvely
    beháviour
Of sílk-sack clóuds! has wílder, wílful-wávier
Méal-drift móulded éver and mélted across skíes?

I wálk, I líft up, I líft up héart, éyes,   5
Down áll that glóry in the héavens to gléan our
    Sáviour;
And, éyes, heárt, what lóoks, what líps yet gáve you a
Rápturous love's gréeting of réaler, of róunder replíes?

And the ázurous hung hílls are his wórld-wíelding
    shóulder
Majéstic—as a stállion stálwart, very-víolet-swéet!— 10
Thése things, thése things were hére and bút the
    behólder
Wánting; whích two whén they ónce méet,
The héart réars wíngs bóld and bólder
And húrls for him, O hálf hurls éarth for him off
    únder his féet.

Commentary: The poem is dated "Vale of Clwyd. Sept. 1, 1877". In a letter to Bridges, for July 16, 1878, Hopkins says:

> "The Hurrahing Sonnet was the outcome of half an hour of extreme enthusiasm as I walked home alone one day from fishing in the Elwy." (LB 56)

1 The time of year is that of harvest, at the end of summer. On either side of the straight road, leading back to St. Beuno's College from the river Elwy, the poet notices the sheaves of reaped corn piled in stooks across the fields, unkempt but beautiful. "Stooks" (or shocks) are groups of sheaves placed upright and supporting each other, so as to permit the drying and ripening of the grain.

2 Looking up to the sky, he admires the movement of the clouds blown before the wind in serried ranks— —as though reflecting in the heavens his own walk along the road.

3 In their texture the clouds seem to combine the contrary qualities of silk-like delicacy and sack-cloth roughness, in a kind of "pied beauty." In their movement there is something wild and wilful, even wanton, like the "barbarous beauty" of the stooks.

4 They drift along the sky like white meal or flour, successively moulding and melting, forming and dissolving again.

5 As for himself, while walking along the road, he lifts up his eyes and heart in rapturous prayer of adoration. The very movement of the line indicates an upward movement, as if the poet would fain rise from the ground "with a fling of the heart", as in WD 3.

6 He even imagines himself moving with the clouds along their "wind-walks," and at the same time over the newly reaped fields, "to glean our Saviour". Here he implicitly recalls the Old Testament story of Ruth, who met Booz while gleaning in his fields and so

became the ancestress of Christ — as St. Matthew records: "Booz begot Obed of Ruth" (i. 5). Similarly, while walking in imagination across the beauty of the heavens, he gleans not any material grain, but Christ himself, who is the "true bread from heaven" (*John* vi. 32).

7   He then turns to address his own eyes and heart, with a characteristic figure of speech, asking them in a spirit of wonder where they have ever received so loving a greeting from looks or lips of man, as this from Christ.

8   In the beauty of the heavens he recognizes the "rapturous love's greeting" of Christ, who is under "the world's splendour and wonder" (WD 5), and whose reply to his prayer is no less real, no less direct than if they were face to face. "Rounder" here has the sense of full, open, unreserved, as in the expression "I will be round with you"; but it also has reference to the round expanse of the sky.

9   Filled with this vision of Christ, he declares that the "azurous hung hills" are as it were the shoulder of Christ, who bears the whole world like another Atlas — "our passion-plunged giant risen" (WD 33). The hills may be those ahead of him, including Maenefa on which St. Beuno's College is situated. But "azurous" and "hung" suggest the sky as seen upside-down against the outline of the hills on the horizon.

10   Such a majestic manifestation of strength reminds him of the "stalwart" form of a stallion, or male horse, and at the same time of the sweet humility of a violet. The words in parenthesis could also read, "like a stallion which is both stalwart and very-violet-sweet." "Violet" refers rather to the flower than to the colour, though the latter might be suggested by the preceding "azurous."

11   He reflects, however, that all this beauty of nature, however impressive, is incomplete without the appreci-

ation of man. So Milton makes Eve ask Adam in
Paradise Lost IV 657:

> "But wherefore all night long shine these, for whom
> This glorious sight, when sleep hath shut all eyes?"

12 It is when nature and man meet together that love
is born in a flash, "like shining from shook foil"
(*God's Grandeur*).

13 Under the impulse of this love, the heart seems to
grow wings, like a dove or carrier-pigeon (cf. *Psalm
liv* and *Cant.* ii. 10). So in WD 3 the poet describes
how he "whirled out wings that spell/ And fled with
a fling of the heart to the heart of the Host."

14 In a final movement of enthusiasm, he feels as if he
can no longer remain on earth. He must needs leap
up to heaven, pushing off—or hurling off—the earth
from under his feet. This is the feeling he notes in
the young lambs which he once observed tossing
themselves about in the fields, in his journal for April
16, 1871:

> "It is as if it were the earth that flung them, not
> themselves." (JP 206)

Only in his case it is he who flings the earth down
from under him. The alliteration with h in this line
effectively echoes the feeling of "hurrah!" expressed
in the title of this poem.

9.

The Caged Skylark

The Caged Skylark

As a dáre-gale skýlark scánted in a dúll cáge
  Man's móunting spírit in his bóne-house, méan
    house, dwélls—
  Thát bird beyónd the remémbering his frée félls;
This in drúdgery, day-lábouring-out lífe's áge.

Though alóft on túrf or pérch or póor low stáge,   5
  Bóth sing sómetimes the swéetest, swéetest spélls,
  Yet bóth droop déadly sómetimes ín their célls
Or wríng their bárriers in búrsts of féar or ráge.

Nót that the swéet-fowl, sóng-fowl, néeds no rést—
Why, héar him, héar him bábble and drop dówn to   10
    his nést,
  But his ówn nést, wíld nést, no príson.

Man's spírit will be flésh-bóund when fóund at bést,
But úncúmberèd: meadow-dówn is nót distréssed
  For a raínbow fóoting it nor hé for his bónes rísen.

Commentary: The poem is dated "St. Beuno's, 1877". It is mentioned in a letter to Bridges for Aug. 8, 1877 (LB 42). The elaborate comparison between a "caged skylark" and the human spirit imprisoned in the body is based on the consideration of the First Exercise in St. Ignatius' *Spiritual Exercises*, "that my soul is imprisoned in this corruptible body".

1 The poet compares the spirit of man to a skylark which, though ready to dare the strongest gales in its upward flight, is now "scanted", or confined, within the limits of a dull cage. The phrase "dare-gale" is coined from the analogy with "dare-devil". There is an effective alliterative contrast between "skylark" and "scanted".

2 Similarly, the spirit of man, which would mount up to heaven, is confined within the dwelling of his body, as a lowly house of bones. "Bone-house" is an Anglo-Saxon kenning (ban-hus), as in *Beowulf* 2508. It is also implied in WD 18: "Ah, touched in your bower of bone...heart," and in WD 1: "Thou hast bound bones and veins in me."

3 Further, the bird can no longer remember the time when he was free to fly above the wild mountain scenery of his "fells"—a word chiefly used of mountains in the Pennines near Stonyhurst.

4 Likewise, the human spirit endures the drudgery of a slave, spending laborious days on earth according to God's curse on Adam: "With labour and toil shalt thou eat thereof all the days of thy life" (*Genesis* iii. 17). There is an echo here of Milton's sonnet *On His Blindness*: "Doth God exact day-labour, light denied?" Only the noun is here used as a verb, with the suffix -out to emphasize the protracted length of time.

5 In the second quatrain, the skylark and the human spirit are now taken together. On the one hand, there are times when they both, despite their confinement, experience a secret joy—whether (as in the case of

the bird) aloft on the turf-lined floor of the cage or on the perch, or (as in the case of man) below on the humble stage of this world, according to the line of Shakespeare: "All the world's a stage" (*As You Like It* ii. 7).

6   In such moments they both sing the sweetest songs— or "spells," in the sense of charming melodies, without the sinister implications of magic. This emphasis on "sweet" recurs in the poem on *The Woodlark*, where, too, "sweet" is connected with "joy".

7   On the other hand, at other times they both experience the weight of this weary world and droop as though in death.

8   Or else they grow frantic in their efforts to escape their prison, with alternating outbursts of fear and anger. "Wring" is a frequent word for suffering in Hopkins' vocabulary; but here it is used in an active rather than a passive sense. "In bursts" recalls "in turns of tempest" in *Carrion Comfort;* while its association with "wring" further points to the sonnet *No worst*.

9   In the sestet, the poet turns his attention to another skylark that is free on his fells. For all his freedom, this bird too needs rest from time to time.

10   After he has babbled his song up there in the sky— "Hear him, hear him," the poet exclaims enthusiastically—he must drop down to his nest, if only to rewind his score (as in *The Sea and the Skylark*).

11   What makes all the difference, however, is that the free bird can repose in his own nest, amid the wilds of nature, not in a prison where he is deprived of his freedom. The sprung rhythm here reinforces the meaning of the words.

12   Similarly, the human spirit, "when found at best" in the final state of resurrection, will be bound by flesh, for such is his nature—composed of body and soul.

13 But then he will feel no encumbrance, no hindrance
from the flesh; no more than the down or fluff of
dandelions, growing to seed in a meadow, feels any
weight from a rainbow. Strictly speaking, "un-
cumbered" should be "unencumbered".

14 The rainbow is said to "foot" the meadow-down, with
one end resting upon it—in a static and transitive
sense, as contrasted with the dynamic and intransitive
sense of "footing" in Milton's *Lycidas*. In the resurrection the "bones risen" are compared to meadow-
down; while the human spirit is the rainbow. The
whole movement of the poem leads up to this triumphant emphasis on "he for his bones risen", which
sums up its main theme.

10.

The Lantern Out of Doors

The Lantern Out of Doors

SÓMETIMES a lántern móves alóng the níght,
  That interésts our éyes. And whó goes thére?
  I thínk; whére from and bóund, I wónder, whére,
With, áll down dárkness wíde, his wáding líght?

Mén go bý me whom eíther béauty bríght   5
  In móuld or mínd or whát not élse makes ráre:
  They ráin agáinst our múch-thick and mársh aír
Rich béams, till déath or dístance búys them quíte.

Déath or dístance sóon consúmes them: wínd
  What móst I may éye áfter, be ín at the énd   10
I cánnot, and óut of síght is óut of mínd.

Chríst minds; Chríst's interest, whát to avów or
        aménd
    There, éyes them, heart wánts, care haúnts, foot
        fóllows kínd,
  Their ránsom, théir rescue, ánd first, fást, last friénd.

Commentary: The poem is generally dated "St. Beuno's 1877". It is partly discussed in a letter to Bridges, for Feb. 15, 1879.

1 The calm reflective mood of this sonnet appears from the first word, "Sometimes", which lacks the immediacy and particularity adopted by the poet in his more enthusiastic moods. Here he describes a common experience in the countryside, as one sits by the window at night and sees a traveller making his way outside, with a lantern to guide his footsteps along the winding path.

2 There is a certain fascination in this moving lantern, which leads the poet to wonder who the traveller is. He even phrases his question like the challenge of a sentry: "Who goes there?" as in the opening words of *Hamlet*.

3 He wonders where the man comes from and whither he is going—with a double question, to which corresponds the double assertion in his unfinished poem: "Thee, God, I come from, to thee go."

4 He continues to revolve such questions in his mind as long as he can see the "wading light", till it merges into the darkness which extends widely in every direction. "Wading" is here used in the sense of OE "wadan", to walk; as in Spenser's *Faery Queene* I i. 12: "Virtue gives herself light, through darkness for to wade." At the same time, the modern sense is not excluded, with the darkness implicitly compared to water.

5 He then goes on to apply this particular experience in the countryside to a more general experience in human relationships. From time to time, he is attracted by the personal beauty of men who pass by him like travellers in the night, their beauty being as it were their lantern.

6 Such beauty may be either "in mould or mind", in body or spirit; or it may be due to some deeper cause

which may well be divine. Here "rare" is used in
the Shakespearean sense of wonderful; as it appears
also in WD 35: "Rare-dear Britain".

7 These persons seem to throw rich beams of light on
the thick, unhealthy atmosphere of our world, which
is compared to a low-lying marsh.

8 But after a time their "rich beams" are all bought
up either by death or at least by distance, so that
they no longer penetrate to us.

9 The poet dwells sadly on the thought of "Death or
distance", by which they are soon consumed, as though
by "devouring time" (cf. Shakespeare's *Sonnet* xix).

10 How eagerly soever he follows the winding steps of
such men as they recede into the darkness, he cannot
"be in at the end"—that is, follow their subsequent
history to its end. The verb of this rather twisted
sentence is "may wind eye after", as Hopkins explains
to Bridges:
   "I mean that the eye winds only in the sense that
   its focus or point of sight winds and that coincides
   with a point of the object and winds with that. For
   the object, a lantern passing further and further
   away and bearing now east, now west of one right
   line, is truly and properly described as winding."
   (LB 66)

11 Once then they go "out of sight", they are soon "out
of mind", as in the familiar English proverb—even
though for a time his thoughts have been wholly
preoccupied with them.

12 Then, in a more optimistic frame of mind, the poet
turns from himself to Christ. Though he may lose
sight of others, and even interest in them, it is not
so with Christ. *He* cares for them, *he* is interested
in them, both to avow what is good and to amend
what is defective.

13 It is Christ who continues to look after them with his eyes, desire them in his heart, pursue them with his loving care, and follow them with his untiring feet; and who ever shows himself kind—not only in the sense of generous, but also in the sense of sharing the same human nature. It is noteworthy that the stresses in this line are mostly on the verbs.

14 Finally, Christ is presented as Our Saviour, who has ransomed and rescued us from sin, and who loves us with a strong, everlasting love, from the beginning to the end. As Jeremias says in the name of God, "I have loved thee with an everlasting love" (xxxi. 3). The final word "friend" emphasizes the truth that the winding of the "lantern out of doors" has its end in the love of Christ.

II.

Oxford, Liverpool, Stonyhurst,

1879-1882

11.

Duns Scotus's Oxford

Duns Scotus's Oxford

TÓWERY cíty and bránchy betwéen tówers;
Cuckoo-échoing, bell-swármèd, lark-chármèd, rook-
  rácked, river-róunded;
The dápple-eared líly belów thee; that cóuntry and
  tówn did
Ónce encóunter in, here cóped and póisèd pówers;

Thou hást a báse and bríckish skírt there, sóurs   5
That néighbour-náture thy gréy béauty is gróunded
Bést in; gráceless grówth, thou hást confóunded
Rúral rúral kéeping—folk, flócks, and flówers.

Yét áh! this aír I gáther and I reléase
He líved on; these wéeds and wáters, these wálls 10
  are whát
He háunted who of áll men most swáys my spírits
  to péace;

Of réalty the rárest-véinèd unráveller; a nót
Rívalled ínsight, be ríval Ítaly or Gréece;
Who fíred Fránce for Máry withóut spót.

Commentary: The poem is dated "Oxford, March 1879,"
after having been (probably) mentioned as "soaking"
in a letter to Bridges for Feb. 22, 1879 (LB 73). It may
be regarded as celebrating the poet's return to Oxford,
after having completed his course of theology at the
St. Beuno's College. What he particularly treasures
in Oxford is the memory of Duns Scotus, the great
mediaeval theologian (1274–1308), whose room is still
to be seen at Merton College. It was during his
residence at St. Mary's Hall, Stonyhurst, that he first
read "Scotus on the Sentences in the Baddely library
and was flush with a new stroke of enthusiasm"—as
he records in his journal for Aug. 3, 1872 (JP 221).

1 The poet first describes the silhouette of Oxford against
the sky, characterized by numerous towers and
branches of trees in between—symbolic of its har-
monious association between "country and town."

2 In summer it echoes to the note of the cuckoo and
the tolling of church-bells, which swarm within its
narrow confines. It is alternately charmed by the
song of the skylark and racked by the cawing of rooks.
It is surrounded by the multiple streams of the Thames
(called Isis as it passes by Oxford) and its tributary
river, the Cherwell.

3 In the river-meadows below the city he pays special
attention to the "dapple-eared lily", as the emblem
of chastity and an example of "pied beauty" in nature.

4 Here in former days, before the Industrial Revolution,
the respective powers of "country and town", nature
and man, met each other, "coped" within the city
walls and "poised" in even balance with each other.
This fruitful tension of "instress" explains the greatness of the university.

5 But "here" is contrasted with "there", as the poet
turns his attention to the "base and brickish" out-
skirts of the "town", growing up in the vicinity of
the gasworks and the railway station.

6 They sour and spoil the natural scenery which has hitherto been close neighbour to the city and the best background for the "grey beauty" of her stone buildings.

7 He therefore rounds on the "graceless growth" with words of indignation, complaining how it has "confounded" the adjoining countryside.

8 He laments the passing of that rural tradition which requires the "keeping", or ceaseless care, of man — with its human "folk", its "flocks" of sheep, and its lovely wild "flowers". His repetition of "rural" is an expression of mourning, as in *Binsey Poplars*:
"Rural scene, a rural scene,
Sweet especial rural scene."

9 In the sestet, however, he revives his spirits with the thought of Duns Scotus, who lived and lectured at the beginning of the fourteenth century in Merton College, adjacent to the Christ Church meadows. The double stress on "Yet ah!" vividly expresses his breathing in of that "cordial air" which makes a hood over the city (*In the Valley of the Elwy*).

10 What makes it all the more cordial for him is that this was the air Scotus himself "lived on". He also pays tender attention to the "weeds", perhaps "the dapple-eared lily" or water-lily, the "waters" of the river Cherwell flowing past them, and the "walls" of the city, as seen from the meadows, extending from Christ Church past Corpus Christi and Merton towards Magdalen College.

11 All this was once frequented—and now "haunted" as if by a ghost—by him whose thought the poet finds most congenial to his spirits.

12 He goes on to describe the contributions of Scotus, the Subtle Doctor, to philosophy and theology. In philosophy, his metaphysical insight was devoted to unravelling the intricate veins of reality by means of

the celebrated "distinctio formalis a parte rei." The
word "realty" here used emphasizes that the reality
is no mere abstraction in the mind, but *real*.

13 This insight was, in Hopkins' opinion, unrivalled,
even in comparison with the great thinkers of ancient
Greece and Rome, or with the more recent Italian
thinker who was his main rival, St. Thomas Aquinas.

14 In theology, his insight was above all vindicated in
his famous defence of the doctrine of the Immaculate
Conception at Paris University, when he filled France
with enthusiasm "for Mary without spot". It is this
ideal which is symbolized in "the dapple-eared lily"
—formerly the national emblem of France (before
it was replaced by the tricolor). Yet there is an
implicit contrast between the lily, which is "dapple-
eared" with the "pied beauty" of nature, and Mary,
who is "without spot", united with him "whose
beauty is past change." Perhaps the poet was here
thinking of the university church dedicated to her,
whose spire is prominent on the skyline of this "towery
city" as viewed from the Christ Church meadow. He
also refers to "the one woman without stain" in WD
30, and to "Mary Immaculate" in *The Blessed Virgin
compared to the Air we Breathe.*

12.

Henry Purcell

Henry Purcell

*The poet wishes well to the divine genius of Purcell
and praises him that, whereas other musicians have
given utterance to the moods of man's mind, he has,
beyond that, uttered in notes the very make and
species of man as created both in him and in all
men generally.*

Have fáir fállen, O fáir, fáir have fállen, so déar
To me, so árch-espécial a spírit as héaves in Hénry
    Púrcell,
An áge is nów since pássed, since párted; wíth the
    revérsal
Of the óutward séntence low láys him, lísted to a
    héresy, hére.

Not móod in hím nor méaning, proud fíre or sácred   5
    féar,
Or lóve or píty or áll that sweet nótes not hís might
    núrsle:
It ís the fórgèd féature fínds me; it ís the rehéarsal
Of ówn, of abrúpt sélf there so thrústs on, so thróngs
    the éar.

Let him óh! with his áir of ángels then líft me, láy
    me! only Í'll
Have an éye to the sákes of him, quaint móonmarks,   10
    to his pélted plúmage únder
Wíngs: so sóme great stórmfowl, whenéver he has
    wálked his whíle

The thúnder-púrple séabeach plúmèd púrple-of-
thúnder,

If a wúthering of his pálmy snow-pínions scátter a
colóssal smíle

Óff him, but méaning mótion fans frésh our wíts
with wónder.

Commentary: The poem is dated "Oxford, April 1879".
It is enclosed with a letter to Bridges dated April 22
of that year, after having been mentioned as "soaking"
in a previous letter for Feb. 22 (LB 73, 80). It represents
Hopkins' first attempt at composing a sonnet in alexandrines; and so he asks his friend in the letter for
April 22:
    "What do you think of the effect of the Alex-
    andrines? That metre unless much broken, as I do
    by outrides, is very tedious." (LB 80)
This sonnet he regards, in a letter for Jan. 4, 1883, as
"one of my very best pieces" (LB 171): and it is inter-
preted by him more fully than any other of his poems,
in answer to Bridges' complaints that it is unintelligible.
The general meaning is explained in this letter:
    "The sonnet on Purcell means this: 1–4. I hope
    Purcell is not damned for being a Protestant, because
    I love his genius. 5–8. And that not so much for
    gifts he shares, even though it shd. be in higher
    measure, with other musicians as for his own indi-
    viduality. 9–14. So that while he is aiming only at
    impressing me his hearer with the meaning in hand
    I am looking out meanwhile for his specific, hie

individual markings and mottlings, 'the sakes of him'. It is as when a bird thinking only of soaring spreads its wings: a beholder may happen then to have his attention drawn by the act to the plumage displayed." (LB 170)

1 The poet goes on in the same letter to explain hst particular meaning of the first lines:

"May Purcell, O may he have died a good death and that soul which I love so much as which breathes or stirs so unmistakeably in his works have parted from the body and passed away, centuries since though I frame the wish, in peace with God! so that the heavy condemnation under which he outwardly or nominally lay for being out of the true Church may in consequence of his good intentions have been reversed." (LB 170-1)

He also discusses the significance of the opening phrase "Have fair fallen" at some length:

"One thing disquiets me: I *meant* 'fair fall' to mean *fair (fortune be) fall*; it has since struck me that perhaps 'fair' is an adjective proper in the predicate and can only be used in cases like 'fair fall the day,' that is, *may the day fall, turn out, fair*. My line will yield a sense that way indeed, but I never meant it so." (LB 171)

He returns to the same point in a letter of Jan. 28, 1883:

"You do not seem quite to have understood my question about *Fair fall*, but whether you understood it or not at any rate you have answered it and set me at rest. The quotation from L.L.L. is decisive.* 'Fair befall your mask' must have the same construction as 'Fair fall the face beneath it'. Now 'fair befall' certainly means 'Fair fortune, all that is fair, nothing but what is fair/ befall' and 'fair'

---

* The quotation is from *Love's Labours Lost* ii. 1 (dialogue between Berowne and Rosaline).

is there a substantive and governs the verb. So
therefore it is and does in 'Fair fall', which is what
I wanted. (*Fair* is of course a substantive in *My
fair* and Shakespeare says 'And every fair from fair
sometime declines'). This being so, I am unwilling
to alter that line, for if it will only stand, it pleases
me much." (LB 173)

Again, in a letter for Feb. 3, 1883, he adds.

"This is a terrible business about my sonnet
'Have fair fallen', for I find that I still 'make myself
misunderstood'. *Have* is not a plural at all, far from
it. It is the singular imperative (or optative if you
like) of the past, a thing possible and actual both
in logic and grammar, but naturally a rare one. As
in the second person we say 'Have done' or in
making appointments 'Have had your dinner before-
hand', so one can say in the third person not only
'Fair fall' of what is present or future but also
'Have fair fallen' of what is past. The same
thought (which plays a great part in my own mind
and action) is more clearly expressed in the last
stanza but one of the *Eurydice*, where you remarked
it." (LB 174)

The relevant stanza from *The Loss of the Eurydice*
reads:

> "And the prayer thou heardst me making
> Have, at the awful overtaking,
>   Heard; have heard and granted
>   Grace that day grace was wanted."

—where the thought, too, is precisely the same as in
this sonnet: a prayer for ultimate salvation. There
is another parallel in Shakespeare's *King John* i. 1:
"Fair fall the bones that took the pains for me!"

2 What is particularly dear to the poet in Henry Purcell
is his "so arch-especial a spirit", just as in the contemporary poem *Binsey Poplars* what he particularly
regrets is "the sweet especial scene", unselved by
"ten or twelve strokes of havoc". Here "arch" is

reminiscent of the "arch and original Breath" in WD 25, and "heaves" looks forward to "My cries heave" in the sonnet *No worst*.

3   "An age", in fact, almost two centuries, has gone by since the great British composer died (1695)—"passed" away, or "parted" from this world.

4   The "outward sentence" which "lays him" low is the decree of excommunication incurred *ipso facto* by all who embrace "a heresy", such as Protestantism. It is "outward" (in scholastic terminology, "material" as opposed to "formal"), inasmuch as the "heresy" is embraced in good faith. In his letter for Jan. 4, 1883, Hopkins explains "Low lays him" as "merely 'lays him low', that is/ strikes him heavily, weighs upon him"; and "listed" as meaning "enlisted" (LB 171).

5   What most impresses the poet in Purcell's music is not so much his "mood" or his "meaning", the "proud fire" in his dancing measures that gives full scope to the human form (cf. *To what serves Mortal Beauty*: "Flung prouder from/ Than Purcell tune lets tread to"), nor, on the other hand, the "sacred fear" of the divine majesty that characterizes his religious music.

6   For such qualities, however impressive, may be "nursled", or fostered, in the "sweet notes" of other composers writing in the same musical style.

7   What he finds—or rather what finds him—in Purcell's music is the "feature" of the composer himself, as it has been "forged" "with an anvil-ding and with fire", namely, the intense labour and the guiding inspiration of musical composition. Cf. *St. Alphonsus Rodriguez*: "On the fighter, forge his glorious day."

8   In other words, what "it speaks and spells" is "*myself*"; it "finds tongue to fling out broad its name" (*As kingfishers*). The epithet "abrupt" has the same force as "sheer" in *That Nature is a Heraclitean Fire*: "Man-shape, that shone/ Sheer off, disseveral, a star". By implication, it also includes the terror of "cliffs of fall

frightful, sheer, no-man-fathomed" in *No worst*. The effect of this music is similar to the thrush's song in *Spring*, which "strikes like lightnings". It impresses and crowds on the ear, as it were "in crisps of curl", like the lark's song in *The Sea and the Skylark*.

9   The sestet is further explained by Hopkins in his letter for May 26, 1879:
   "The sestet of the Purcell sonnet is not so clearly worked out as I could wish. The thought is that as the seabird opening his wings with a whiff of wind in your face means the whirr of the motion, but also unaware gives you a whiff of knowledge about his plumage, the marking of which stamps his species, that he does not mean, so Purcell, seemingly intent only on the thought or feeling he is to express or call out, incidentally lets you remark the individu-alising marks of his own genius." (LB 83)
Here "air" has the double meaning of song (as used in the sixteenth and seventeenth centuries) and atmosphere. The poet is evidently thinking at once of the hymn of the angels at Christ's nativity (*Luke* ii. 13) and of Donne's poem *Aire and Angels*. The gram-matical structure has the sense: However much his angelic melody may transport me with its rise and fall, I will only pay attention to "the forged feature" implicit in it.

10 Just as the poet winds "eye after" "beauty bright in mould or mind" in *The Lantern out of Doors*, so he will "have an eye" only to "the sakes" of Purcell himself. This term he explains in his letter for May 26, 1879:
   "Sake is a word I find it convenient to use: I did not know when I did so first that it is common in German, in the form *sach*. It is the *sake* of 'for the sake of', *forsake, namesake, keepsake*. I mean by it the being a thing has outside itself, as a voice by its echo, a face by its reflection, a body by its shadow, a man by his name, fame, or memory, *and also* that in the thing by virtue of which especially

it has this being abroad, and that is something distinctive, marked, specifically or individually speaking, as for a voice and echo clearness; for a reflected image light, brightness; for a shadow-casting body bulk; for a man genius, great achievements, amiability, and so on. In this case it is, as the sonnet says, distinctive quality in genius." (LB 83)

In a subsequent letter for Aug. 14, 1879, he corrects himself, noting that "that German word is *sache*, not *sach*, except in compounds" (LB 85). He is later apologetic for his use of the word in his letter for Jan. 4, 1883:

"'Sakes' is hazardous: about that point I was more bent on saying my say than on being understood in it." (LB 171)

He has already used the word, in its singular form, in WD 22: "Five! the finding and sake/ And cipher of suffering Christ./ Mark, the mark is of man's make." Here, too, he goes on to speak of "quaint moonmarks", which he also explains in his letter for May 26, 1879:

"By *moonmarks* I mean crescent shaped markings on the quill-feathers, either in the colouring of the feather or made by the over-lapping of one on another." (LB 83)

He adds in his letter for Jan. 4, 1883:

"The 'moonmarks' belong to the image only of course, not to the application; I mean not detailedly: I was thinking of a bird's quill feathers." (LB 171)

Similarly, with reference to man, he speaks (in *That Nature is a Heraclitean Fire*) of "his firedint, his mark on mind". The bird's plumage is, moreover, described as "pelted," which may mean a) serving as his "pelt" or skin, b) protecting him like a "pelt" or shield, or c) fixed in his skin like darts "pelted" at him.

11 The movement of the poet's imagination is through "angels" and "pelted plumage under wings" to "some great stormfowl"—a seabird, such as the stormy petrel, which has braved a storm at sea. The formation is

akin to the "sweet-fowl, song-fowl" of *The Caged Skylark*. The "stormfowl" is the grammatical subject of "fans" in the final line—with a temporal and a conditional clause intervening.

12 He presents the bird strutting along the beach, reflecting on its plumes, while the sand also reflects, the dark purple glow from the thunder-clouds. His description recalls the "glow, glory in thunder" of WD 5.

13 Against this vivid background the poet notes the sudden inscape, as it were spreading "a colossal smile off him", when a mighty gust of wind blows on his snowy wings. "Wuthering" is explained in his letter for May 26, 1879, as "a Northcountry word for the noise and rush of wind; hence Emily Bronte's 'Wuthering Heights'" (LB 83). "Palmy" may refer either to palm-branches, or to the palm of the hand; but it has a further meaning of triumphant, as in *Hamlet* i. 1: "In the most high and palmy state of Rome." The "colossal smile" looks forward to *My own heart*, where the poet casts for the comfort of God, "whose smile...unforeseen times...lights a lovely mile".

14 The bird, while "meaning motion", intending flight, "fans fresh our wits with wonder," fills our minds with a vivid impression of wonder. Cf. the contrasting use of "fan" in *Carrion Comfort*, where the background is also one of tempest, but the mood is dark.

13.

The Candle Indoors

The Candle Indoors

SOME cándle cléar burns sómewhere I cóme bý.
I múse at hów its béing puts blíssful báck
With yéllowy móisture míld night's bléar-all bláck,
Or tó-fro ténder trámbeams trúckle at the éye.

Bý that window what tásk what fíngers plý,   5
I plód wóndering, a-wánting, júst for láck
Of ánswer the éagerer a-wánting Jéssy or Jáck
There/Gód to aggrándise, Gód to glórifý.—

Come yóu indóors, come hóme; your fáding fíre
Mend fírst and vítal cándle in clóse heart's váult: 10
You thére are máster, dó your ówn desíre;

What hínders? Áre you béam-blind, yét to a fáult
In a neíghbour déft-hánded? are yóu that líar
And, cást by cónscience óut, spendsávour sált?

Commentary: The poem is dated "Oxford, 1879", and more precisely from a letter to Bridges for June 22, 1879, where the poet speaks of it as "a companion to the Lantern, not at first meant to be though, but it fell in" (LB 84). The situation here is exactly opposite to that in *The Lantern out of Doors*: there the poet was indoors and looking outside, here he is outside and looking in at a window.

1 In this case, the poet is himself walking "all down darkness wide", like the stranger in *The Lantern out of Doors*, and he notices the light of a candle burning within a house. His thoughts are much influenced by Portia's words in *The Merchant of Venice* v. 1:
    "That light we see is burning in my hall.
    How far that little candle throws his beams!
    So shines a good deed in a naughty world."

2 He goes on to muse and ponder on the nature of the light: how its existence serves to restrain or keep in check the menacing blackness of the night. Here "blissful", like "clear" above, is an adjective used partly in a predicative sense with "being" (its blissful being), partly in an adverbial sense with "puts back" (puts blissfully back).

3 It does so by means of its yellow flame, whose "moisture" is fed by the liquefying wax of the candle. The blackness of night is said to "blear all", that is to blur the outlines and varied colours of nature, as in *Spelt from Sibyl's Leaves* (cf. "bleared, smeared with toil" in *God's Grandeur*). The "mild" night suggests the time of spring, as in *In the Valley of the Elwy*.

4 He then observes the way the candle seems to send out beams of light, that flicker to and fro with the slightest movement of the eyelids, "truckling" to the eye as a slave truckles to, obeys every whim of his master. The word "trambeam" includes many associations: a) a beam of light, as in sunbeam or moonbeam; b) a tree, as in "whitebeam" (*The Starlight Night*), or piece of timber, as mentioned by Christ in

the Sermon on the Mount (*Matthew* vii. 3-5) and developed by the poet in l. 12 of this sonnet; c) the Latin word for "beam" in this sense, as used in the Vulgate translation, is "trabs", which suggests "tram" in sound; d) "tram" has further reference to tram-lines, which already existed in Hopkins' day; e) it may also be a thread of silk, or "tram-silk," used for the weft of the best silk cloth.

5 He proceeds to wonder who is the person he sees "by that window" and what is the task at which he seems so busily engaged.

6 "Plod" suggests a slow and pensive movement, as he passes the house. His thought also prompts a desire.

7 This desire is all the keener as his curiosity remains unsatisfied. The uncommon form of comparative in "eagerer" is used by way of alliteration with "answer", and thus reinforces the meaning of the line. As for the object of his curiosity, he cannot even discern if the person at the window is male or female, "Jessy or Jack"—inverting the usual order and replacing Jill with Jessy for the sake of the rhythm.

8 As for the object of his desire, it is for the person, whoever he or she is, to give glory to God—as he does in *God's Grandeur* and *Pied Beauty*.

9 He breaks off, however, in the sestet to rebuke himself, after the manner of the final point in St. Ignatius' Meditation on the Kingdom in the *Spiritual Exercises*. As so often in his poems, he addresses his own heart, urging himself to attend first to "that being indoors each one dwells" (*As kingfishers*), and to remain "home at heart" (*To what serves Mortal Beauty?*). It is his first duty to glorify God himself, before urging this on others.

10 It is his primary responsibility to rekindle the "fading fire" of divine love in his own heart (cf. Shakespeare's "thy fading mansion" in *Sonnet* cxlvi), to tend to the "candle" of life burning in the "close vault" of his

own heart. The phrase "vital candle" recalls Othello's famous speech (which reappears in *That Nature is a Heraclitean Fire*):

> "Put out the light, and then put out the light;
> If I quench thee, thou flaming minister,
> I can again thy former light restore,
> Should I repent me; but once put out thy light,
> Thou cunning'st pattern of excelling nature,
> I know not where is that Promethean heat
> That can thy light relume. When I have pluck'd
>   the rose,
> I cannot give it vital growth again." (v. 2)

11   In the home of his heart he is master; there he can do his own desire; but for other people he cannot answer.

12   He therefore asks what hinders him, rebuking himself in words derived from Christ's Sermon on the Mount, as already suggested by the pun on "beam". He should not be blind to the beam in his own eye, like the hypocrite in Christ's parable.

13   While being "deft-handed," or skilful, in removing the smallest motes in the eye of his neighbour,

14   he must look out for himself, lest—as Christ warns in *Matthew* v. 13—the "salt" of his faith loses its savour, and he becomes good for nothing save to be cast out by his own conscience and trodden underfoot by men. Here the epithet "spendsavour" is coined by analogy with "spendthrift."

14.

The Handsome Heart

The Handsome Heart

at a Gracious Answer

'But téll me, chíld, your chóice; whát shall I búy
You?'—'Fáther, whát you búy me Í like bést.'
With the swéetest áir that sáid, still plíed and préssed,
He swúng to his fírst poised púrport óf replý.

Whát the héart is! whích, like cárriers let flý— 5
Doff dárkness, hóming náture knóws the rést—
To its ówn fine fúnction, wíld and sélf-instréssed,
Falls líght as tén years lóng taught hów to and whý.

Mánnerly-héarted! móre than hándsome fáce—
Béauty's béaring or múse of móunting véin, 10
Áll, in thís case, báthed in high hállowing gráce...

Of héaven what bóon to búy you, bóy, or gáin
Not gránted!—Ónly...O ón that páth you páce
Run áll your ráce, O bráce stérner that stráin!

Commentary: The poem is dated generally "Oxford, 1879", and more precisely from a letter to Bridges for June 22, 1879, in which it is enclosed together with *The Candle Indoors*. Of them both Hopkins says they are "capable of further finish. I am afraid they are not very good all through." This he describes as "historical, autobiographical, as you would say, or biographical" (LB 84). In a subsequent letter for Aug. 14, 1879, he expresses surprise at his friend's "liking this sonnet so much. I thought it not very good." He goes on to recount its occasion:

> "The story was that last Lent, when Fr. Parkinson was laid up in the country, two boys of our congregation gave me much help in the sacristy in Holy Week. I offered them money for their services, which the elder refused, but being pressed consented to take it laid out in a book. The younger followed suit; then when some days after I asked him what I shd. buy answered as in the sonnet. His father is Italian and therefore sells ices. I find within my professional experience now a good deal of matter to write on." (LB 86)

Later on, in a letter for Oct. 8, 1879, he tells Bridges that "the little hero of the Handsome Heart has gone to school at Boulogne to be bred for a priest and he is bent on being a Jesuit" (LB 92). In addition to a revised version, which Hopkins sent his friend in August, 1879, he recast the sonnet in the longer alexandrine lines; but it was the original version that Bridges decided to publish in 1918, and subsequent editors have concurred with his decision. Bridges also made use of it in his own poem *The Spirit of Man*.

1   The poet, speaking to the younger boy, urges him to make his choice and say what he would like to have with the money. The opening phrase echoes the title of Southwell's poem *A Child My Choice*, and the concluding line of *Spring*: "Most, O maid's child, thy choice and worthy the winning."

2 The boy, speaking to the poet as priest, addresses him as "Father", and leaves the choice in his hands, as a point of good manners.

3 The past participles here conceal a difference of construction: "that said" is an ablative absolute, for "that having been said by him", while "plied and pressed" are participles agreeing with "he swung" in the next line—with the implication of "for an answer".

4 The more he was pressed in one direction for an answer, the more "he swung" back, like a pendulum, to his original position. While containing the image of a pendulum, "poised" has the further meaning of weighed, deliberate. Cf. its use in WD 21: "Thy unchancelling poising palms were weighing the worth."

5 The poet exclaims on the mystery of the human heart, as in WD 18: "O unteachably after evil, but uttering truth." He likens it to a carrier-pigeon, which, once released from the cage, can find its way home, as also in WD 3: "My heart, but you were dove-winged, I can tell, carrier-witted, I am bold to boast."

6 In parenthesis, he notes that, once the "darkness" of original sin is removed, the "homing nature" of man instinctively "knows the rest", that is to say, the right way to "God who is our home" (Wordsworth, *Immortality Ode*). The idea of "doff darkness"—as one might remove an impediment of clothing—is repeated from *The Loss of the Eurydice*: "Doffs all, drives full for righteousness."

7 The heart "falls light", that is, turns readily, to its proper task, which is to love the supreme good—according to the scholastic teaching that the object of the will is good in general. This movement of the heart is "wild", or natural, and "self-instressed", or spontaneously issuing into act.

8 The verb "falls," while bearing the literal sense of turns, attends, may also imply a movement of gravity, not downwards, but upwards — according to the

Augustinian saying: "Amor meus, pondus meum"—
"My love, my weight". "Light" is also used in the
sense of readily, as an adverb, and with the implication of upwards, in contrast to heavy. The "ten
years" indicate the boy's age, during which time he
has been "taught" by his parents "how to" behave
in accordance with his true nature and "why"—for
the love of God.

9 In the sestet, the poet goes on to point out the significance of his title, that "handsome is as handsome
does", and "more than handsome face" is "the handsome heart",—of one who observes good manners not
merely in outward form, but from an inward motive.
This idea is also developed in a contemporary letter
to Bridges, dated Oct. 22, 1879, where the poet discusses
different kinds of beauty—that of the body, which
he calls "dangerous" (as in *To what serves Mortal
Beauty?*), that of the mind, which is greater and "not
to call dangerous", and above all, that of character,
which is precisely the "handsome heart" (LB 95).

10 He looks, "in this case", beyond the beauty of outward "bearing" or behaviour, and that of the inward
mind or "muse of mounting vein". Here "mounting"
has the meaning of "ascending", and "muse" is the
spirit or poetic genius, as in Shakespeare's *Henry V*
i. Prol.: "O for a muse of fire, that would ascend
the brightest heaven of invention!" "Vein" has the
meaning of "tendency" or "spirit".

11 He finds all this in the boy, but "bathed" in the higher
beauty of "hallowing" or sanctifying grace—"God's
better beauty, grace" (*To what serves Mortal Beauty?*).
The same image of "bathed" is to be found in WD
23: "To bathe in his fall-gold mercies."

12 The poet wonders "what boon", or bountiful gift, he
should "buy" of heaven with the bidding of prayer
(cf. *The Starlight Night*), or what "gain", or goodly
addition, that should not straightway be "granted".
He is here perhaps thinking of Desdemona's words to

Othello: "I wonder in my soul what you could ask me that I should deny"—where she also speaks of a "boon" (iii. 3).

13 He breaks off at "Only . . ."—reflecting, as in *Spring*, how the "innocent mind and Mayday in girl and boy" may all too readily "cloy", "cloud" and "sour with sinning". Hence he concludes with a prayer, that the boy may continue to run the whole of his earthly race along the same path as at present. This image is taken from St. Paul's *I Corinthians* ix. 24: "So run that you may obtain", with an echo perhaps of Donne's *Holy Sonnet*, "This is my play's last scene", which continues: "And my race . . . hath this last pace."

14 For this purpose he urges the boy to "brace" or gird himself with all his energy for the stern trials of life. The "strain" refers both to his natural tendency, which is a "strain of the earth's sweet [being in the beginning" (*Spring*), and to the voluntary effort or "fire of stress" (WD 2) required of him in time of adversity.

15.

Andromeda

Andromeda

NÓW Tíme's Andrómeda on thís rock rúde,
With nót her eíther béauty's équal ór
Her ínjury's, looks óff by bóth hórns of shóre,
Her flówer, her píece of béing, doomed drágon fóod.

Time pást she has béen attémpted ánd pursúed   5
By mány blóws and bánes; but nów hears róar
A wílder béast from Wést than áll were, móre
Rífe in her wróngs, more láwless, ánd more léwd.

Her Pérseus línger and léave her tó her extrémes?—
Píllowy áir he tréads a tíme and hángs   10
His thóughts on hér, forsáken thát she séems,

All whíle her pátience, mórselled ínto pángs,
Mounts; thén to alíght disárming, nó one dréams,
With Górgon's géar and bárebill/ thóngs and fángs.

Commentary: The poem is dated "Oxford, Aug. 12, 1879". It is mentioned by Hopkins in a letter to Bridges for Aug. 14, 1879:

> "I enclose a sonnet on which I invite minute criticism. I endeavoured in it at a more Miltonic plainness and severity than I have anywhere else. I cannot say it has turned out severe, still less plain, but it seems almost free from quaintness and in aiming at one excellence I may have hit another." (LB 87)

Its subject is derived from the Greek legend of Perseus and Andromeda, which had been the subject of a poem by Charles Kingsley. Andromeda, daughter of Cepheus and Cassiopeia, had been chained to a rock on a lonely island as food for a sea-monster, in punishment for her mother's offence against the sea-god, Poseidon (Neptune). But Perseus came to her rescue on his return from slaying the Gorgon, Medusa, and turned the monster to stone by showing it the Gorgon's head. The poet here interprets the legend as an allegory of Christ (Perseus) and the Church (Andromeda), where the latter is seen as waiting for her Lord to come and save her from the dangers of this world. He may also have been thinking of the Christian legend of St. George and the Dragon, with allegorical reference to England.

1 The poet begins by speaking of the Church as "Time's Andromeda", in that she renews the experiences of Andromeda throughout time. He also emphasizes the fact that she is no mere legendary figure of the past, but a present reality here and "now." He shows her "on this rock rude", the rock of Peter (*Matt.* xvi. 18), which is continually buffeted by the waves of this world. "This rock" could also be England, whose heavenly patron is St. George.

2 He notes how she is unequalled both in spiritual beauty (as described in the *Song of Songs*) and in undeserved suffering.

3 From her rock she looks out to sea in mingled fear

of the monster and hope of her Saviour. The two "horns of shore" indicate two promontories on either side of the bay, while suggesting the metaphorical "horns" of her dilemma as she awaits the monster.

4 At stake is her "flower" of maidenhood, that "innocent mind and Mayday in girl and boy" which Hopkins compares in *Spring* to "a strain of the earth's sweet being in the beginning in Eden garden". "Piece" is here used in a Shakespearian sense, with reference to a rare woman, such as Marina in *Pericles* iv. 2 and the Princess Elizabeth in *Henry VIII* v. 5. "Dragon food" is the poet's own correction of "dragon's food" in his previous version. "Dragon" is a traditional description of the devil, as in *Revelation* xii, where he is shown pursuing the Woman.

5 The poet now looks back over "time past", recollecting how the Church has been variously subjected to vexation ("attempted" in the sense of "tempted") and persecution ("pursued", as in the above-mentioned passage of *Revelation*).

6 "Blows and banes" express in alliterative form the various misfortunes suffered by the Church, both from natural and from supernatural causes. Cf. "dark heaven's baffling ban" and "hell's spell" in the sonnet *To seem the stranger.*

7 Now, however, he finds her menaced by a "wilder beast" than any in the past, akin to the beast with seven heads described in *Revelation* xiii and the "beast of the waste wood" mentioned in WD 20. Coming out of "the black West" (*God's Grandeur*), it may be identified with the growing forces of agnosticism and materialism, in the context of the industrial revolution.

8 From this beast she suffers more injuries than she has ever suffered before. The adjective "rife" is normally used either absolutely, as in the sonnet *To seem the stranger,* "where wars are rife," or followed by "with".

9 In the sestet, the poet enters into her thoughts, as she waits anxiously for the coming of Christ, "her Perseus", wondering why he lingers and leaves her to her fate—as when he lingered on his way to heal Lazarus (*John* xi). "Her extremes" recalls the similar situation of the nun in WD 28: "He was to cure the extremity where he had cast her". The grammatical form of "linger and leave" may be explained by the omission of "will" or "can" at the beginning of the line.

10 He then turns his attention to Christ, who is now in heaven, since his ascension, treading "pillowy air" until the day of his second coming. Similarly, Perseus came to the rescue of Andromeda, flying through the air on the winged sandals of Hermes (Mercury).

11 He has not forgotten her, however forsaken she may seem in her present desolation, but "hangs his thoughts on her". Cf. Hamlet's "Why, she would hang on him" (i. 2).

12 All this while her patience, divided as it were into morsels or separate moments of pain and "schooled at forepangs" (*No worst*), paradoxically "mounts" up in hope to meet him. These two lines significantly anticipate the later "terrible" sonnets.

13 There follows an effective juxtaposition of the mounting patience of the Church with the alighting of Christ to rescue her. In a manner "no one dreams" —beyond human understanding—he looses the "thongs" that bind the maiden and overcomes the "fangs" of the monster. "Disarming" is thus used in a double sense, for freeing the one and overpowering the other.

14 Just as Perseus slew the monster "with Gorgon's gear and barebill", the armour and exposed beak of Medusa, so Christ will appear at the end of the world and cast terror into the hearts of the Church's enemies. "Barebill" may mean either exposed beak, as of a bird, or unsheathed sword or pike: perhaps

both meanings are here intended by the poet. The caesural mark after "barebill" indicates a pause to separate the prepositional phrase from the object of "disarming".

16.

Peace

Peace

Whén will you éver, Péace, wild wóoddove, shý
    wings shút,
Your róund me róaming énd, and únder bé my
    bóughs?
When, whén, Peace, wíll you, Péace? I'll nót play
    hýpocríte

To ówn my héart: I yíeld you dó come sómetimes;
    bút
That píecemeal péace is póor peace.   What púre   5
    péace allóws
Alárms of wárs, the dáunting wárs, the déath of ít?

O súrely, réaving Péace, my Lórd should léave in líeu
Some góod! And só he dóes leave Pátience éxquisíte,
That plúmes to Péace thereáfter. And whén Peace
    hére does hóuse
He cómes with wórk to dó, he dóes not cóme to cóo,   10
           He cómes to bróod and sít.

Commentary: The poem is dated "Oxford, 1879." A previous draft is dated Oct. 2 of the same year. It is a "curtal sonnet", like *Pied Beauty*, but in alexandrines (with six stresses to the line). It may be regarded as a companion poem to *Patience*.

1 The poet addresses his words to the Spirit of Peace, whom he presents under the traditional form of a dove —the bird that returned to Noah's ark with an olive branch as a sign that the flood was over (*Gen.* viii. 11). He describes this bird as a "wild wooddove", which is "shy" of approaching him with its "wings shut", and is easily alarmed, like the "flake-doves sent floating forth at a farmyard scare" in *The Starlight Night*. The grammatical construction is either an ablative absolute, "with your shy wings shut", or the first part of the main clause, "(when will you ever) shut your shy wings..."

2 Thinking of himself as a tree in the wood, he asks the dove of Peace when he will ever cease flying around and settle quietly beneath his boughs. The transposition of "under" and "be" is prompted by the need of a parallel phrase with "round me". "Round me roaming" is as it were a single word, the object of "end".

3 He repeats his question "when", and invokes Peace twice, as though with plaintive insistence. His manner is reminiscent of his invocation to the Holy Spirit on a similar occasion in *No worst*: "Comforter, where, where is your comforting?" The repetition of "Peace" likewise recalls the repetition of "Patience" in the companion poem. On the other hand, he wants to be fair and to avoid exaggeration in his complaint, dramatizing his plight as though he had never received any gifts from Peace. "Play hypocrite" has thus the literal meaning of acting a part, instead of being himself.

4 "Own my heart" is explained by Hopkins himself, in a letter to Bridges for Aug. 21, 1884, as

"merely 'my own heart', transposed for rhythm's sake and then *tamquam exquisitius*, as Hermann would say." (LB 196)

He admits, "yields" the point, that Peace does come to him from time to time.

5 But such peace as he experiences is only "piecemeal", like the "morselled" patience of *Andromeda*. The thought of this line is based on punning contrasts between "piece" and "peace", "poor" and "pure". "Pure peace" is not "piecemeal", but whole and entire.

6 His condition resembles, rather, that of the last times prophesied by Christ, when there shall be "wars and rumours of wars" (*Matt.* xxiv. 6). "Pure peace" is incompatible with "alarms" of possible wars, still less with the "daunting" or intimidating effect of actual wars, which are "the death of" peace.

7 In the sestet, however, he turns from words of complaint to considerations of comfort. Surely, he reflects, if God "reaves" me of Peace, he must leave some other good "in lieu"—instead. The precise meaning of "reaves" is explained in the above-mentioned letter to Bridges, as "rob, plunder, carry off" (LB 196).

8 Again, he refuses to "play hypocrite", and readily admits that God does leave Patience in place of Peace. Here the epithet "exquisite" corresponds to "rare" in the sonnet on *Patience*, as well as to the "delicious" quality of "kindness".

9 He thinks of Patience as a newly-hatched chick, which becomes the "wooddove" of Peace when it is fully-fledged or "dovewinged" (WD 3)—with "pride" of "plume" like the *Windhover*. Such perfect Peace is only realized "thereafter" in the future life of heaven. Meanwhile, here on earth, the Peace that is born of Patience does not "house" or dwell in man without further condition.

10 He comes not merely "to coo", to soothe the troubled heart with divine consolation as with a foretaste of Paradise, but "with work to do", to prompt man to further activity in the divine service. This is a traditional piece of advice for the time of consolation: not to rest in it as if it were an end, but to make use of it as a means of spiritual progress.

11 He comes "to brood and sit", like a mother bird over the eggs in her nest until they are hatched and then fully fledged. Thus true Peace is essentially productive, though not necessarily in an active sense. Here "to coo" is employed not merely in contrast, but also as concomitant with "to brood and sit", implying the contemplative life.

17.

Felix Randal

Felix Randal

FÉLIX RÁNDAL the fárrier, O is he déad then?
    my dúty all énded,
Who have wátched his móuld of mán, big-bóned and
    hárdy-hándsome
Píning, píning, till tíme when réason rámbled in it
    ánd some
Fátal fóur disórders, fléshed there, áll conténded?

Síckness bróke him. Impátient, he cúrsed at fírst,   5
    but ménded
Béing anóinted and áll; though a héavenlier héart
    begán some
Mónths éarlier, since Í had our swéet repríeve and
    ránsom
Téndered to him. Áh well, God rést him áll road
    éver he offénded!

This séeing the síck endéars them tó us, us tóo it
    endéars.
My tóngue had táught thee cómfort, tóuch had   10
    quénched thy téars,
Thy téars that tóuched my héart, child, Félix, poor
    Félix Rándal;

How fár from thén forethóught of, all thý more
    bóisterous yéars,
When thóu at the rándom grim fórge, pówerful
    amídst péers,
Didst féttle for the gréat grey dráyhorse his bríght
    and báttering sándal!

Commentary: The poem is dated "Liverpool, April 28, 1880." It was enclosed in a letter to Bridges for June 18, 1880. The lines of the sonnet are alexandrine. Here we find another instance of what Hopkins remarks in a previous letter for Aug. 14, 1879: "I find within my professional experience now a good deal of matter to write on" (LB 86).

1 The poet begins at the end of his story, with the news of the death of Felix Randal and his own reaction: "O is he dead then?" His duty, as a priest, to visit this sick member of his flock is also at an end. A "farrier" is a blacksmith who specializes in shoeing horses (Lat. *ferrarius*, from *ferrum*, iron).

2 He describes the "lovely manly mould" (*The Loss of the Eurydice*) of the farrier, with characteristic emphasis on his handsome appearance and physical strength. Cf. also "the man, handy and brave" in WD 16.

3 There is a striking contrast between his former health and his present "pining" in sickness, even to the stage of delirium, "when reason rambled" in "his mould of man"—that is to say, his wits seemed to wander from their proper place.

4 Some four different types of sickness, fatal to his life, were "fleshed" or embodied in him, and "contended" for mastery over him. The number "four" may have reference to the four elements or corresponding humours of the body, which are said to "contend" with each other in times of stress; as in *Hamlet* iv. 1: "Mad as the sea and wind, when both contend which is the mightier", *Macbeth* ii. 2: "Death and nature do contend about them, whether they live or die", and *King Lear* iii. 1: "Contending with the fretful elements". The idea of "fleshed" is that the disorders are somehow incarnate in the sick man; just as the Son of God was "heart-fleshed" in Mary (WD 34).

5 The sturdy farrier was broken by sickness, both in

body and in spirit; but after his first reaction of impatience, he "mended" in spirit on being "anointed" with the sacrament of the dying, extreme unction.

6   The addition of "and all" is a characteristic Irish expression, which the poet may well have learnt from the lips of Felix Randal himself—Randal being an Irish name, and Liverpool largely Irish in population. He then qualifies his previous statement by saying that the change of heart in his patient had begun "some months earlier".

7   This was when he first brought communion—the sacrament of the eucharist—to him in hospital, no doubt, after hearing his confession. He calls the sacrament "our sweet reprieve and ransom" from sin, as being the memorial of the sacrifice Christ offered for our redemption on Calvary. Similarly, in *The Lantern out of Doors* Christ is described as "their ransom, their rescue".

8   "Tendered" combines the meaning of brought, offered, with the association of tender, delicate; as in WD 31: "Lovely-felicitous Providence / Finger of a tender of, O of a feathery delicacy". The poet then turns from these past memories to the present fact, with a sigh of "Ah well", and a prayer for the soul of the departed, "God rest him". Cf. *The Starlight Night*: "Ah well! it is all a purchase, all is a prize"; and the words of old Gobbo in *The Merchant of Venice* ii. 2: "God rest his soul!" The idiom "all road ever" is North country dialect for "in whatever way he may have", "however he may have".

9   In the first part of the sestet, the poet reflects on his experience at the hospital, how in visiting the sick there he comes to be fond of them, and they in turn of him. At the end of the line, "to them" is implied after "endears".

10 As priest, he had spoken words of comfort to the

patient, and with his hand he had soothed him in his grief.

11 All the same, the tears which he sought to quench with the touch of his hand, had touched his own heart with pity for this strong man now reduced to weakness. The word "child" refers both to the condition of Felix Randal as a patient, and to his spiritual relationship to the priest.

12 He goes on to reflect on the "more boisterous years" of the farrier, when he was far from the "forethought" of this fatal illness. In this line "of" is without object; but it is sufficiently clear from the context. "Then" is intruded between "from" and "forethought", as though replacing a definite article, and is in apposition to "thy more boisterous years": i.e. How far were you then, during your years of vigour, from any forethought of sickness or death!

13 Then he plied his task "at the random grim forge" —"random" in the sense of built with irregularly shaped stones, while implying the thoughtless, carefree labour of the man himself. There, too, he displayed his Herculean power and "forged his glorious day" (*St. Alphonsus Rodriguez*) "with an anvil-ding" (WD 10). "Amidst peers" has a comparative force: more than other men.

14 Thus the poet moves from the news of the farrier's death to the picture of him at work in his smithy, forging the horseshoe for "the great grey drayhorse." Here "fettle" has the meaning of prepare, make ready, together with the implication that both the farrier and the horse are "in fine fettle". A "drayhorse" is a large, powerful horse employed in pulling heavy loads. His horse-shoe is described as a "sandal" that is "bright" in its new appearance and "battering" in its heavy, clattering sound upon the road.

18.

As kingfishers catch fire

As kingfishers catch fire

As kíngfishers cátch fire, drágonflies dráw fláme;
  As túmbled óver rím in róundy wélls
  Stones ríng; like éach tucked stríng tells, éach
    hung béll's
Bow swúng finds tóngue to flíng out bróad its náme;
Each mórtal thíng does óne thing ánd the sáme: 5
  Déals out that béing índoors éach one dwélls;
  Selves—góes itsélf; *mysélf* it spéaks and spélls,
Crying *Whát I dó is mé: for thát I cáme.*

Í say móre: the júst man jústicés;
  Keeps gráce: thát keeps áll his góings gráces;   10
Ácts in God's éye whát in God's éye he ís—
  Chríst—for Chríst pláys in ten thóusand pláces,
Lóvely in límbs, and lóvely in éyes not hís
  To the Fáther thróugh the féatures of mén's fáces.

Commentary: The poem is undated, and is mentioned in none of the poet's letters. Without title, it is yet the most characteristic expression of Hopkins' aesthetic philosophy in poetic form, as influenced by the Scotist theory of "this-ness" (*haecceitas*).

1   From the outset, the poet uses particular illustrations from the world of nature to bring out the "instress" present in its many "inscapes". He first contemplates a kingfisher diving to catch a fish in a river or pond, while its brightly coloured wings catch a glint of sunlight and "flash out" (*God's Grandeur*). He also notes a similar phenomenon in the dragonflies skimming about over the surface of the water, as they seem to "draw flame" into their irridescent wings.

2   Passing from light to sound, he speaks of stones that are pushed over the "rim" or edge of round wells and "ring" out from the depths as they hit against the sides and the dry bottom. The Hopkinsian form, "roundy", emphasizes the quality of roundness by smoothing out the rhythm of the line; cf. *Duns Scotus's Oxford*: "Towery city and branchy between towers". The thought of these two lines is echoed in Hopkins' notes on the "Contemplation for Obtaining Love":

> "All things therefore are charged with love, are charged with God, and if we know how to touch them give off sparks and take fire, yield drops and flow, ring and tell of him." (SD 195)

3   The sound of ringing stones suggests the musical metaphor, first, of a string instrument, such as a harp or 'cello, which when plucked or "tucked" gives out a characteristic note; and, secondly, of a bell "hung" in the belfry of a church, whose sound has many echoes in the poetry of Hopkins.

4   The bell's "bow" is the thickened side of the bell which is struck by the "tongue" or clapper within as it moves this way and that, and flings out the sound peculiar to itself, which is for the poet its proper

"name". He is here alluding to the European custom of "christening" bells with a proper name, and also perhaps recalling the old nursery rhyme:

"'Oranges and lemons', say the bells of St. Clement's;
'When will you pay me', say the bells of Bow Bailey;
'When I am rich', say the bells of Shoreditch."

5 After giving the above illustrations, the poet goes on to enunciate his general philosophical theory. All things on earth have but one thing to do, each in its own manner, as it were fulfilling its proper mission in life. There is a certain emphasis (though not metrical) on "does", connected with Hopkins' theory of "pitch" as defined in his spiritual writings:

"*Pitch* is ultimately simple positiveness, that by which being differs from and is more than nothing and not-being, and it is with precision expressed by the English *do* (the simple auxiliary), which when we employ or emphasize, as 'he said it, he did say it', we do not mean that the fact is any more a fact but that we the more state it. . . . So that this pitch might be expressed, if it were good English, *the doing* be, *the doing* choose, *the doing* so and so in that sense. . . . And such 'doing-be', and the thread or chain of such pitches or 'doing-be's, prior to nature's being overlaid, is self, personality." (SD 151)

6 In other words, each thing "deals out" or gives expression to that peculiar quality or pitch of being which dwells "indoors each one". "Deal" is a favourite word of Hopkins, used in the sense of giving or distributing, which is the characteristic action of good—"Bonum est diffusivum sui" (Good is diffusive of itself). Cf. *To what serves Mortal Beauty?*: "God to a nation dealt that day's dear chance".

7 This is the quality of selfhood, individuality, "this-ness", which the poet emphasizes in accordance with Scotus' theory of "haecceitas". In order to stress the action expressive of selfhood, he coins the verb

"selves", in the sense of "goes itself", goes its own way, reveals and realizes itself.

8 Each thing echoes, on its own level of pitch, the words spoken by Christ, the Word of God, to Pilate: "For this I was born, and for this I came into the world, that I might bear witness to the truth" (*John* xviii. 37).

9 In the sestet, the poet develops the theology implicit in his aesthetic theory, with special reference to man. Just as "each mortal thing" utters itself according to the order of nature, so in the order of grace each "just man justices"—that is, fulfils all justice in his actions, as Jesus said to John the Baptist: "For so it becomes us to fulfil all justice" (*Matt*. iii. 15).

10 For by the very fact that the just man is, by definition, in a state of grace, "all his goings"—all his movements and actions—are graces in the sight of God. In theological terminology, the grace that he "keeps" is habitual, or *sanctifying*, grace; while the graces that characterize "all his goings" are *actual* graces. The original version of these lines was more regular in rhythm; viz.

"Then Í say móre: the júst man jústicés;
Keeps gráce and thát keeps áll his góings gráces."

11 He lives and moves in the presence of God, acting outwardly what he is within, in all sincerity, without hypocrisy, according to the teaching of Christ in the Sermon on the Mount (*Matt*. vi). The emphasis on "acts" is due to a revision of the original text, which originally read: "In God's eye acts". . . .

12 That is to say, he lives and moves in Christ, as St. Paul says of himself to the Galatians: "I live, now not I; but Christ lives in me" (ii. 20). For Christ is not only a human individual, who lived and died two thousand years ago in Palestine, but the God-man, who lives on in his members in all places and at all times, "even to the consummation of the world" (*Matt*. xxviii. 20). The verb "plays", with "to the Father"

two lines below, recalls the description of divine Wisdom in *Proverbs* viii. 30-1:

"I was with him, forming all things, and was delighted every day, playing before him at all times, playing in the world; and my delights were to be with the children of men."

13 The poet sees Christ in the "limbs" and "eyes" of men, in so far as men are members of his Mystical Body—according to the frequent teaching of St. Paul. He has the same idea in his spiritual writings:

"For grace is any action, activity, on God's part by which, in creating or after creating, he carries the creature to or towards the end of its being. . . . It is Christ in his member on the one side, his member in Christ on the other. It is as if a man said: That is Christ playing at me and me playing at Christ, only that it is no play but truth; That is Christ *being me* and me being Christ." (SD 154)

14 It is not merely that Christ is present in just men as his members, but he looks through their features "to the Father"—as he is Son of God by nature, and they are sons by adoption (cf. *Romans* viii. 14-17).

19.

Ribblesdale

Ribblesdale

ÉARTH, sweet Éarth, sweet lándscape, with léavès
   thróng
And lóuchèd lów grass, héaven that dóst appéal
To, wíth no tóngue to pléad, no héart to féel;
That cánst but ónly bé, but dóst that lóng—

Thou cánst but bé, but thát thou wéll dost; stróng   5
Thy pléa with hím who déalt, nay dóes now déal,
Thy lóvely dále down thús and thús bids réel
Thy ríver, and ó'er gives áll to ráck or wróng.

And whát is Earth's éye, tóngue, or héart else, whére
Élse, but in déar and dógged man?—Áh, the héir   10
To his ówn selfbént so bóund, so tíed to his túrn,

To thríftless réave both our rích róund world báre
And nóne réck of world áfter, thís bids wéar
Earth bróws of súch care, cáre and déar concérn.

Commentary: The poem is dated "Stonyhurst, 1882", and
is mentioned in a letter to Bridges for Mar. 26, 1883,
as a companion to *In the Valley of the Elwy* (LB 178).
Like that poem, it is based on a contrast between
"Ribblesdale"—the valley of the river Ribble, which
flows past Stonyhurst College to the town of Preston
—and the work of man, the "inmate" who "does not
correspond" to the beauty of his surroundings. It is
also enclosed in a letter to R. W. Dixon for June 25,
1883, with an epigraph from *Romans* viii. 20:
>   "Vanitati enim creatura subjecta est, non volens
>   sed propter eum qui subjecit eam in spe" cum
>   praecc. et sqq. (LD 108)

1 The poet begins by addressing the earth, with reference
   to the whole natural landscape of the Ribble valley,
   which is no less dear to him than the "sweet special
   rural scene" of *Binsey Poplars*. It reminds him of
   "the earth's sweet being in the beginning in Eden
   garden" (*Spring*), with the rich foliage of its trees.
   "Throng" he explains in his letter to Dixon as "an
   adjective as we use it here in Lancashire" (LD 109):
   it has the sense of thronged or massed together.

2 He also explains "louched" as "a coinage of mine and
   is to mean much the same as *slouched, slouching*"
   (LD 109). He thinks of the earth as bowing down in
   a mute appeal to heaven for vengeance against the
   injustice of man.

3 Yet the earth has "no tongue to plead" her cause,
   as Hopkins pleads his in the sonnet *Thou art indeed
   just*, and "no heart to feel" her injuries, which are
   comparable to those of Time's *Andromeda*.

4 Without reason (as in man) and sensation (as in
   animals), earth has but being, in which she outlasts
   both man and animals.

5 Turning to the second quatrain, the poet repeats the
   previous line, with a further stress on the being of
   earth, which is not only long-lasting, but good—

according to the scholastic axiom: "Omne ens est bonum" (All being is good).

6 It is this very being of earth which strengthens her plea against the vandalism of that man who has "dealt" and is even now dealing a dolorous blow to the loveliness of the dale. This blow seems to consist in some ugly factory that has been built on the banks of the Ribble for mere material profit. Cf. "the stroke dealt" in WD 6.

7 "Down" follows "deal", in the sense of dealing a stroke down on the victim. The river is thus made to "reel" under the impact of the blow, perhaps with the excess of impure waste products poured into it from the factory. The same concatenation of words recurs in Hopkins' explanation of *The Sea and the Skylark* in his letter to Bridges for Nov. 26, 1882:

> "The lark in wild glee races the reel round, paying or dealing out and down the turns of the skein or coil right to the earth floor." (LB 164)

8 Thus man gives earth over to rack and ruin by his wrongful dealing.

9 Yet the poet reflects in the sestet that Earth is not, after all, without "eye, tongue, or heart".

10 Her sight, speech and feeling are to be found precisely in man who does her so much wrong—man who is both "dear", for his natural gifts of reason and free will, and "dogged" or obstinate, with his heart "unteachably after evil" (WD 18); cf. WD 9: "Wring thy rebel, dogged in den, man's malice." Man is "the heir" to the kingdom of God, as St. Paul notes in *Romans* viii. 17.

11 Yet he overlooks his eternal destiny, in his narrow selfishness and search for material gain. "Selfbent" recalls "the bent world" in *God's Grandeur*, where "bent" has the sense of evil inclination. "Turn" means material advantage, as in *Othello* i. 1: "I follow him to serve my turn upon him" (Iago).

12 He is quite "thriftless", or reckless of the future, in reaving bare, or plundering, the riches of this round world; and no place is safe from his depredations. Here "thriftless" is an adjective used as an adverb.

13 Meanwhile, like Macbeth, he is prepared to "jump the life to come" (i. 7). The same complaint is made in *God's Grandeur* and in a similar context: "Why do men then now not reck his rod?" The grammar of these two lines is somewhat obscure. "Reave" and "reck" are grammatically parallel to each other, as infinitives of consequence dependent on "*so* bound, *so* tied to his turn", with "as" implied—"so as to reave ...and none reck...." "Both" ought, strictly speaking, to be placed before "thriftless", while "none" has the force of "not" or "nothing".

14 It is this evil inclination in man which makes Earth wear "brows of such care," contracting her natural beauty into unseemly wrinkles and furrows. Similarly, Byron in *Don Juan* vi. 6 speaks of "the brow of earth" as "wrinkled by the sins and tears" of men. Her "care and dear concern" is for "her bonniest, dearest to her, her clearest-selved spark, Man" (*That Nature is Heraclitean Fire*).

III.

Dublin, 1885-1889

20.

To what serves mortal beauty?

To what serves mortal beauty?

To whát serves mórtal béauty ǀ —dángerous; dóes
set dánc-

cing blóod—the O-séal-that-só ǀ féature, flung próuder
fórm

Than Púrcell túne lets tréad to? ǀ Sée: it does thís:
keeps wárm

Men's wíts to the thíngs that áre; ǀ what góod
means—whére a glánce

Máster more máy than gáze, ǀ gáze out of cóunte-   5
nánce.

Those lóvely láds once, wét-fresh ǀ wíndfalls of
wár's stórm,

How thén should Grégory, a fáther, ǀ have gléanèd
élse from swárm-

èd Róme? But Gód to a nátion ǀ déalt that dáy's
dear chánce.

To mán, that néeds would wórship ǀ blóck or bárren
stóne,

Our láw says: Lóve what áre ǀ love's wórthiest,   10
wére all knówn;

World's lóveliest—mén's selves.   Sélf ǀ fláshes off
fráme and fáce.

What dó then? hów meet béauty? ǀ Mérely méet
it; ówn,

Hóme at heart, héaven's sweet gíft; ǀ then léave,
lét that alóne.

Yea, wísh that thóugh, wish áll, ǀ God's bétter
béauty, gráce.

Commentary: The poem is dated "Aug. 23, 1885". It is an unusual form of sonnet, using alexandrines (i.e. six stresses per line), and noting a caesura in each line to divide the stresses into three on either side.

1 The poet begins by asking the question which serves as title to his poem: What is the purpose of "mortal beauty", as distinct from the immortal beauty of God, or divine grace? He immediately goes on to explain why he asks this question at all. There is a certain danger in such beauty, as he points out in a letter to Bridges, dated Oct. 22, 1879:

> "I think no one can admire beauty of the body more than I do, and it is of course a comfort to find beauty in a friend or a friend in beauty. But this kind beauty is dangerous." (LB 95)

2 The blood of man is set dancing, or throbbing, by lovely features that prompt one to exclaim: "O seal that so!" —i.e. Keep it just as it is now! This phrase is perhaps suggested by Hamlet's description of his father:

> "A combination and a form indeed,
> Where every god did seem to set his seal,
> To give the world assurance of a man." (iii. 4)

Hopkins may also have been thinking of Florizel's declaration to Perdita in *The Winter's Tale* iv. 3: "When you speak, sweet, I'd have you do it ever..." The image of "dancing blood" seems to come from the same play, where Leontes finds his heart dancing through jealousy (i. 2).

3 There is something deeply stirring in this "human form divine" (Blake), when displayed in its native splendour or "pride"—so that even the dancing measures of the great British composer, Henry Purcell, fail to do full justice to it. Cf. Hopkins' admiration of the "proud fire" of this favourite composer of his in the sonnet *Henry Purcell*. He then proceeds to answer his question in a conversational manner, as it were taking his reader by the sleeve and pointing: "See: it does this."

4   His explanation is that mortal beauty serves to draw
    the attention of man to "realty"—to "the things that
    are". It lends a warmth of feeling and interest to
    the otherwise cold regard of human reason. It shows
    "what good means", since beauty is the outward
    manifestation of goodness, or in scholastic terminology
    the "splendor formae"—as when we say a handsome
    person is "good-looking".

5   He adds, however, that a simple "glance" may take
    in more of reality, may "master more", than a long
    "gaze"—even, or especially, when this is protracted
    into a "gaze out of countenance" (causing the other
    person to blush or look aside). The reason is that a
    glance is enough to recognize the divine essence in
    in man, whereas a gaze takes in the human limitations
    and gives rise to human temptations.

6   By way of illustration, he recalls the story—recorded
    in Bede's *Ecclesiastical History*—of England's con-
    version to Christianity in the reign of Pope St. Gregory
    the Great. Before he became Pope, Gregory was
    walking in the "swarmed" market-place of Rome,
    and there he noticed two fair boys on sale as slaves.
    On learning that they were English boys, who had
    been taken prisoner in war, he remarked: "Non
    Angli, sed Angeli!"—Not Angles, but Angels! The
    poet compares these "lovely lads" to apples blown
    down in a storm and picked up from the ground as
    "windfalls", wet and fresh. He opens the sentence
    with the object of "gleaned", as it is their beauty
    which is the main point of his illustration.

7   Had they not been fair, Gregory would not have
    noticed them amid the crowds of the market-place, or
    "gleaned" them from the ground—as Hopkins gleaned
    "our Saviour" from the heavens in *Hurrahing in
    Harvest*.

8   It was through "that day's dear chance", given or
    "dealt" to the English nation by God in his "lovely-
    felicitous providence" (WD 31), that Gregory became

"a father" to England by sending a band of mission-
aries under St. Augustine for her conversion to the
faith.

9 In the sestet, the poet draws a moral conclusion, after
noting the deep instinct in man to worship some
object, be it only some "block" of wood or "barren
stone". In the latter expression he is thinking of the
idols of the gentiles, as characterized in *Isaiah* xliv,
Wisdom xiii, and *Psalm* cxv.

10 His conclusion is the Christian law of love, as declared by St. Paul in *Romans* xiii. 10: "Love is the
fulfilment of the law". The love of man should be
directed to what is worthiest of love, not in the outer
world of matter, but in the inner world of self—
what he calls the "clearest-selved spark" of nature in
That Nature is a Heraclitean Fire. The parenthetical
"were all known" recalls the similar parentheses in
WD 6: "And few know this", and in *Pied Beauty*:
"Who knows how?" In style it is akin to the manner
of Langland's *Piers Plowman*, which Hopkins regarded
as a precursor of his "sprung rhythm".

11 Once again, therefore, he lays characteristic emphasis
on "men's selves" as what is "loveliest" in nature;
for it is "self" that "flashes" out, like "shining from
shook foil" (*God's Grandeur*), from the "frame and
face" of men. And through this self of man he
catches sight of the deeper self of Christ; for, as he
notes in *As kingfishers*:
    "Christ plays in ten thousand places,
  Lovely in limbs, and lovely in eyes not his
  To the Father through the features of men's faces."

12 But there still remains the practical question: What
are we to do about it? How are we to "meet beauty"
in practice? His answer is simple: "Merely meet it"
—just that and no more.

13 We should recognize it—"own" in the sense of admit
—as the "sweet gift" of heaven, without losing our

heart to something that is merely mortal. "Home at heart" is in inverted order for "(keeping) heart at home". Then we should leave it alone, without pursuing it with a desire that is too easily clouded and sours "with sinning" (*Spring*).

14 Yet he adds that we may lawfully "wish" it, as we may lawfully "wish all", to be crowned and fulfilled by the "better beauty" of God which is "grace". For this is, in scholastic terminology, the love, not of "concupiscence", but of "benevolence", which is akin to divine love. Thus the whole movement of the poem leads up from "mortal beauty" to the "better beauty" of God.

21.

(The Soldier)

(The Soldier)

YES. Whý do we áll, séeing of a sóldier, bléss him? bléss

Our rédcoats, our társ? Bóth these béing, the gréater párt,

But fráil clay, náy but fóul clay. Hére it ís: the héart,

Since, próud, it cálls the cálling mánly, gíves a gúess

That, hópes that, mákesbelíeve, the mén must bé no   5 léss;

It fáncies, féigns, deems, déars the ártist áfter his árt;

And fáin will fínd as stérling áll as áll is smárt,

And scárlet wéar the spírit of wár thére expréss.

Mark Chríst our Kíng. He knóws war, sérved this sóldiering thróugh;

He of áll can réeve a rópe best. Thére he bídes in blíss   10

Now, and séeing sómewhere some mán do áll that mán can dó,

For lóve he léans forth, néeds his néck must fáll on, kíss,

And crý 'O Chríst-done déed! So Gód-made-flésh does tóo:

Were Í come ó'er agáin' cries Chríst 'it shóuld be thís'.

Commentary: The poem is dated "Clongowes, Aug. 1885".
It is composed in alexandrines, like the preceding poem.
Its thought-structure is based on the traditional analogy
between the life of a soldier and the service of Christ,
which goes back to St. Paul, as in *II Tim.* ii. 3:
"Endure hardships as a good soldier of Jesus Christ".
For Hopkins, as a Jesuit, this analogy would have been
suggested by St. Ignatius' Meditation on the Kingdom
of Christ in the *Spiritual Exercises*, which also appears
in *The Windhover* and WD 35.

1 From the beginning, the poet adopts a conversational
tone, as it were agreeing with the unexpressed remark
of some hidden interlocutor: "Yes"—it is indeed as
you say. But for Hopkins this simple answer has
further, theological resonances, as being the characteristic response of man to the offer of Christ the King
—as in WD 2: "I did say yes". This resonance is
here supported by the rhyme word "bless" repeated
twice in the second half of the line. He is, however,
not content with merely agreeing that we all admire
a soldier when we see him; but he goes on to ask
why this is so. The unusual idiom, "seeing of a
soldier", may be derived from "catching sight of a
soldier"; or else it may be partitive—something of,
even if only a glimpse.

2 By "soldier" he means not only the "redcoats", or
those in the British Army, but also the "tars", or
those in the British Navy. In either case, the question
"why" is a natural one, seeing that both are, for "the
greater part", weak human beings.

3 They are, like ourselves, "but frail clay"—mortal
men, formed like Adam out of earth (*Gen.* ii. 7)—
"nay but foul clay"—sinners, who have added of
their own to Adam's original sin. The question
stated, the poet at once proceeds to give the answer:
"Here it is"—in much the same colloquial manner
as in *To what serves Mortal Beauty?*: "See: it does
this".

4 We naturally regard the military profession, or "calling", as a "manly" one, and our heart feels a sentiment of pride in it.

5 We therefore guess, or hope, or at least pretend to ourselves, that the individual soldiers correspond to the ideal of their profession.

6 We imagine, pretend, consider, like to think that "the artist"—here used in the widest sense of the word, as one who follows a profession or technique—possesses the ideal quality attaching to his art. As we expect the priest to be holy, the scholar to be learned, the lawyer to be prudent, so we expect the soldier to be brave. "Feigns" was a later insertion by the poet, replacing "it" in the original line: "It fancies, it deems".

7 Hence we readily imagine that the soldier is as "sterling" within—that is, firm and reliable, as the English pound sterling used to be—as he is "smart", or neatly dressed, without. "Fain" is altered from the original version: "So feigns it finds"—in keeping with the alteration of the previous line.

8 We likewise imagine that as he wears the "scarlet" uniform of a "redcoat", he also wears "the spirit of war" expressed by this colour, the colour of blood. Strictly speaking, "wear" should have the singular form "wears"; but it seems that the poet has shifted the number in view of the grammatical ambiguity of the subject "all", so as to preserve the assonance between "wear" and "war". "Express" is used for "expressed", as "throng" is used for "thronged" in *Ribblesdale*, thus giving an effect of compactness and strength.

9 In the sestet, the poet characteristically turns to "Christ our King", as in the second part of St. Ignatius' Meditation on the Kingdom. He begins with "Mark", in an arresting tone of voice, as in WD 22: "Mark, the mark is of man's make". He notes that

Christ has himself been through the hardship of "war" and "soldiering" to which he calls us, according to the words St. Ignatius puts into his mouth:

"Whoever shall wish to come with me must be content to eat as I do, and so to drink and dress, etc. as I do. In like manner, he must labour as I do by day, and watch at night, etc. so that in like manner afterwards he may share with me in the victory."

10 As a sailor, too, "he of all can reeve a rope best"—literally, pass the end of a rope through a ring, or rope together. That is to say, Christ, as "master of the tides" (WD 32), is preeminent on sea, as well as on land. In WD 12, Hopkins uses this metaphor in the sense of throwing out a rope to save those struggling in the waters: "The millions of rounds of thy mercy not reeve even them in?" This is what Christ has done for men drowning in the waves of this world, by his death on Calvary—"Hither then, last or first, to hero of Calvary, Christ,'s feet...men come" (WD 8). Now he "bodes but abides" (WD 32) in heavenly bliss; while he continues to follow earthly events with close interest.

11 Whenever he sees somewhere on earth "some man do all that man can do"—that is to say, in cooperation with divine grace, for without it man can do nothing—

12 Christ "leans forth" out of heaven in his condescending love, like the "blessed damozel" in D.G. Rossetti's poem: "The blessed damozel leaned out/ From the gold bar of heaven". He must needs fall on the neck of that man and embrace him, as he did in the mediaeval legend of St. John Gualbert, who forgave his enemy and was embraced by the figure of Christ from the crucifix above the altar.

13 Such a "deed", performed in a moment of "stress" of being, is as it were done by Christ himself, who is God made man—not only individual as man, but also universal by reason of his divine immensity.

14 Indeed, if Christ were to return to earth at this very
    moment, *this* is precisely what he would be doing—
    namely, doing "all that man can do". The final
    emphasis on "this" indicates, with a glance at the
    Scotist theory of "haecceitas", the peculiar character
    of the Christ-like action. The double repetition of
    'cry" is partly prompted by the alliteration with
    "Christ", and partly used to reinforce the enthusiastic
    feeling of the climax.

22.

(Carrion Comfort)

(Carrion Comfort)

NOT, I'll nót, cárrion cómfort, Despáir, not féast on
    thée;
Not untwíst—sláck they may bé—these lást stránds
    of mán
In me ór, most wéary, crý *I cán no móre.* I cán;
Can sómething, hópe, wish dáy come, nót choose nót
    to bé.

But áh, but Ó thou térrible, whý wouldst thou rúde   5
    on mé
Thy wríng-world ríght foot róck? lay a líonlimb
    agáinst me? scán
With dárksome devóuring éyes my brúisèd bónes?
    and fán,
O in túrns of témpest, me héaped there; me frántic
    to avóid thee and flée?

Whý? That my cháff might flý; my gráin lie, shéer
    and cléar.
Nay in áll that tóil, that cóil, since (séems) I kíssed   10
    the ród,
Hand ráther, my héart lo! lapped stréngth, stole jóy,
    would láugh, chéer.
Cheer whóm though? the héro whose héaven-handling
    flúng me, fóot tród
Me? or mé that fóught him? O whích one? is it
    éach one? That níght, that yéar
Of nów done dárkness Í wretch lay wréstling with-
    (my Gód!) my Gód.

Commentary: The poem is undated, but is probably one of the two sonnets mentioned in a letter to Bridges for May 17, 1885, as written "after long silence" (LB 219). It is the first of the series of "terrible" sonnets composed in Dublin during this year. Also, like several of the preceding poems, its lines are all alexandrines.

1 The title of the poem, "carrion comfort", is taken from the expression in the opening line, which means carnal pleasure or delight. This is for Hopkins the equivalent to despair, which he personifies with a capital D; since it is the resort of one who gives up hope of heavenly comfort, or spiritual consolation. It is to Despair, the Giant in Bunyan's *Pilgrim's Progress*, that he addresses his first words, indignantly rejecting the temptations of the flesh with a triple "not". "Feast" is reminiscent of Fortinbras' exclamation at the end of *Hamlet*: "O proud Death! What feast is toward in thine eternal cell?" (v. 2)

2 The "last strands of man" in him—the "bones and veins" that God has bound in him (WD 1), together with the fibres of his spiritual being "laced with fire of stress" (WD 2)—may now be slack, as he feels his vital energy ebbing away, but he refuses to "untwist" what Donne calls "that subtle knot which makes us man" (*The Extasie*), by yielding to temptation.

3 In his weariness, recalling that of Hamlet, he is tempted to cry out: "I can no more!"—in the manner of Chaucer. But he replies almost savagely to this temptation with the flat assertion: "I can!"

4 There is something he can do. He can cling to the hope that a new day of consolation will dawn, according to the advice of St. Ignatius in his *Rules for the Discernment of Spirits* (first series, rule 8):

"Let him who is in desolation labour to be in patience, contrary to the vexations that come to him; and let him think that he will soon be consoled."

At the very least, he can "not choose not to be", by

resisting the temptation to despair and thereby giving
a positive answer to Hamlet's question: "To be or
not to be" (iii. 1).

5 In the words that now follow, he turns to address not
Despair, but Christ, who is as it were "throned
behind" despair—even as he was present to the nun
in "the unshapeable shock night" (WD 29). At first,
however, he sees Christ as a "terrible" monster, in
much the same way as he confessed his "terror" on
a similar occasion in WD 2.

6 He feels himself rocked to and fro in a "rude", yet
strangely gentle manner (cf. WD 16: "Dandled the to
and fro"), by that right foot which wrings the world
with a "chief woe, world-sorrow" (*No worst*). He
wonders why Christ treats him thus, menacing him
as a lion menaces his victim—he being the "lion of
Judah" (*Revelation* v. 5).

7 He wonders why this lion scans his "bruised bones"
with eager eyes that seem ready devour him in an
instant. Here he is perhaps thinking of Shakespeare's
Sonnet xix: "Devouring Time, blunt thou the lion's
paws."

8 Then, varying the Biblical metaphor, he feels Christ
—as Job felt God (*Job* xxxviii. 1)—coming upon him
in the mighty gusts of a whirlwind, and winnowing
him heaped there like a pile of wheat on the threshing-
floor. His thought is from the preaching of John the
Baptist, as given in *Matthew* iii. 12:
    "Whose fan is in his hand; and he will thoroughly
    cleanse his floor and gather his wheat into the barn.
    But the chaff he will burn with unquenchable fire."
Before this mighty wind, he is "frantic to avoid" the
divine visitation and to "flee"—like the dead leaves
before the unseen presence of the West Wind in
Shelley's *Ode*.

9 In the sestet, he summarizes the questions of the
preceding four lines with a simple repetition of

"Why?" His answer is no less simple: "That my chaff might fly; my grain lie". It is a simple matter of the separation of "black, white; right, wrong", as foreshadowed by the coming of night in *Spelt from Sibyl's Leaves.*

10 "Nay"—there is more to it than this. Through his sufferings, he is not only purified of his chaff-like imperfections, which are blown away by the "tempest" of divine wrath, but fortified by an unsuspected joy in his very act of kissing the rod—that is, of accepting God's punishment. This is the act of saying "yes" at "lightning and lashed rod" (WD 2), which prompts him to ask: "Why do men then now not reck his rod?" (*God's Grandeur*) The proverbial phrase, to "kiss the rod", occurs twice in Shakespeare: in *Two Gentlemen of Verona* i. 2, and in *Richard II* v. 1. He recognizes the hand of God amid the "toil and trouble" (*Macbeth* iv. 1), amid the "mortal coil" (*Hamlet* iii, 1) or commotion, of his disturbed feelings.

11 What he "kissed" was not merely the "rod", but rather the "hand" of God holding it; and so what before seemed to be the "lightning" of wrath, now turns out to be the warmth of "love" (cf. WD 9). He even feels like laughing and cheering, "hurrahing" for very joy.

12 But whom is he to cheer? Is it "the hero", Christ, who "flung" him down as though from heaven, whose foot "trod" him down "with a horror of height (WD 2)? Christ is also referred to as "hero" in WD 8 and 35, and in *The Loss of the Eurydice.*

13 Or is it he himself, who dared to fight with Christ, as Jacob fought all night with the Angel of the Lord at Bethel (*Genesis* xxxii. 24)? Is it not, perhaps, each side—both Christ and himself—that he is really cheering, recognizing beneath the outer conflict an inner unity?

14 He recalls it as a particular occasion of darkness

many years ago ("now done")—perhaps the same occasion as that mentioned in WD 2—when he felt himself wrestling in his mind with (blasphemous though it may sound) no less an adversary than God. "That night, that year" may perhaps be paraphrased as "that night which seemed a year in duration"; cf. *I wake and feel*: "But when I say hours I mean years." In the culminating repetition of "my God", there is a striking contrast of tone from one to the other: from a sudden feeling of horror at his own audacity, to an act of humble adoration before God.

23.

No worst, there is none

No worst, there is none

NÓ worst, there ís none. Pítched past pítch of gríef,
Móre pangs will, schóoled at fórepangs, wílder wríng.
Cómforter, whére, whére is your cómfortíng?
Máry, móther of ús, whére is your relíef?
My críes heave, hérds-long; húddle in a máin a chíef-   5
woe, wórld-sorrow; on an áge-old ánvil wínce and
    síng—
Then lúll, then léave off. Fúry had shríeked 'No
    líng-
ering! Lét me be féll: fórce I múst be bríef'.
O the mínd, mínd has móuntains; clíffs of fáll
Fríghtful, sheer, nó-man-fáthomed. Hóld them chéap   10
Máy who ne'er húng there. Nór does lóng our smáll
Dúrance déal with that stéep or déep. Here! créep,
Wretch, únder a cómfort sérves in a whírlwind: áll
Life déath does énd and éach day díes with sléep.

Commentary: The poem, which is undated, is probably that mentioned—together with *Carrion Comfort*—in a letter to Bridges for May 17, 1885, from University College, Stephen's Green, Dublin:

> "I have after long silence written two sonnets, which I am touching: if ever anything was written in blood one these was." (LB 219)

It has nothing of the spiritual joy recalled in the sestet of *Carrion Comfort*, but it expresses the state of desolation, in terms of an elaborate "underthought" from *King Lear* Act IV (cf. FL 252-3).

1 In the opening line, the poet applies to himself the the sentiments of Edgar on seeing his blinded father, Gloucester, wandering over the heath led by an old man:

> "O gods! Who is't can say, 'I am at the worst'?
> I am worse than e'er I was...
> And worse I may be yet; the worst is not
> So long as we can say, 'This is the worst'." (iv. 1)

Each moment he feels he has reached the limit of pain, only to find that there is no such limit. His sufferings seem to have risen to a level or "pitch of grief" far above the normal.

2 Yet the preceding "forepangs" only prepare the way for further "pangs" that "wring" his being in even "wilder" fashion. The use of "wring" in this context looks back to its similar use in WD 9 and *Carrion Comfort*.

3 He looks in vain for heavenly comfort, first, to the Holy Ghost, the Paraclete or "Comforter", repeating the insistent question, "Where?"—as in WD 3.

4 He next turns to Mary, who is mother of Christ and spiritual mother of all Christians. In the Litany of Loreto, she is invoked as "Comforter of the afflicted".

5 He goes on to describe his sufferings in a series of disconnected metaphors. First, he associates his heaving cries with the movement of a herd of cattle

along a country lane, their ungainly backs heaving up and down the whole length of the herd, until they huddle together at the gate of the field they are to enter. Secondly, he is reminded of the sea ("main" in its secondary meaning), whose waves likewise heave up and down; for the sea is a traditional symbol of sorrow and woe, like the "high flood" in WD 7.

6   Here he recognize his own private sorrow as but part of "a chief woe", a "world-sorrow". In "chief" there is probably a reference to Christ, as Head of the Church (Fr. "chef", Lat. "caput"), in connection with St. Paul's teaching in *Colossians* i. 18–24; since it is in his Passion that the "stroke dealt" by God has its "swelling" and "high flood" (WD 7). Thirdly, he turns to the auditory metaphor of the sound of iron on a black-smith's anvil, as it seems to "wince and sing"—to flinch and ring out—under the repeated blows of the hammer. This recalls the "anvil-ding" of WD 10, with the added sense of "age-old", as in *Spring and Fall*: "It is the blight man was born for".

7   Finally, he connects this sound with the whistling of a violent storm, which now rises to a shriek, now falls to a lull and seems to "leave off" for a time. In the shriek of the storm, reminiscent of *King Lear* Act III, the poet hears as it were the voice of a Fury, one of the Erinyes or Eumenides of Greek legend.

8   It is a voice clamouring for immediate vengeance and unrestrained cruelty within a brief period of time. Here "fell" has the meaning of cruel; and "force" is perforce, of necessity.

9   In the sestet, the poet draws yet more freely on the imagery of *King Lear*, particularly Act IV Sc. 6, where Edgar, disguised as a peasant, leads his blind father in imagination to the cliffs of Dover and gives him a vivid description of the dizzy fall. Thus he reflects that the mind, too, has its mountains, its places of danger, where one feels "trod hard down with a horror of height" (WD 2).

10   The very words he uses echo the phraseology of
Edgar:
>   "How fearful
> And dizzy 'tis to cast one's eyes so low!
> . . . Halfway down
> Hangs one that gathers samphire, dreadful trade!
> . . . I'll look no more
> Lest my brain turn, and the deficient sight
> Topple down headlong."   (iv. 6)

"No-man-fathomed" also echoes Edgar's "So many
fathom down precipitating".

11   Only those despise such fearful experiences who know
them merely from hearsay, and have never "hung
there" like Edgar's "one that gathers samphires".

12   In any case, the weakness of man cannot long endure
such terrible experiences; cf. Kent's words at the end
of *King Lear*: "The wonder is he hath endur'd so
long" (v. 3). As T. S. Eliot points out in *Burnt Norton*,
"human kind cannot bear very much reality", whether
of ecstasy or of horror.

13   Turning away, therefore, from the "horrible steep"
of the cliff, the poet seeks a shelter analogous to that
which the faithful Kent found for Lear on the stormy
heath:
> "Gracious my lord, hard by here is a hovel;
> Some friendship will it lend you 'gainst the
>   tempest. . .
> Here is the place, my lord; good my lord, enter;
> The tyranny of the open night's too rough
> For nature to endure."   (iii. 2, 4)

In calling himself "wretch", he also recalls Lear's
famous speech before entering the hovel:
> "Poor naked wretches, wheresoe'er you are,
> That bide the pelting of this pitiless storm. . ."
>   (iii. 4)

The expression "a comfort serves" is equivalent
to "such comfort as serves", with a characteristic
omission of the relative pronoun subject. The storm

is here called a "whirlwind", with reference to *Job* xxxviii. 1, where God speaks to Job "out of the whirlwind".

14 Finally, the poem is rounded off with yet another Shakespearian allusion, appropriately from *The Tempest*: "Our little life is rounded with a sleep" (iv. 1). Just as death brings an end to the troubles of life, or "this mortal coil" (*Hamlet* iii. 1), so "each day dies with sleep". Such an ending seems rather pessimistic; but at least the poet looks to a respite from pain, which is all he can do in the circumstances. His final word on the subject is to be found in his subsequent poems.

24.

To seem the stranger

To seem the stranger

To séem the stránger líes my lót, my lífe
Amóng strángers. Fáther and móther déar,
Bróthers and sísters áre in Chríst not néar
And hé my péace / my párting, swórd and strífe.

Éngland, whose hónour O áll my héart woos, wífe   5
To mý creáting thóught, would néither héar
Me, wére I pléading, pléad nor dó I: I wéar-
y of ídle a béing but bý where wárs are rífe.

I am in Íreland nów; now Í am at a thírd
Remóve. Nót but in áll remóves I cán   10
Kind lóve both gíve and gét. Ónly what wórd

Wísest my héart breeds dárk heaven's báffling bán
Bars ór hell's spéll thwarts. Thís to hóard unhéard,
Héard unhéeded, léaves me a lónely begán.

Commentary: The poem is undated, but is probably one of the four sonnets which "came like inspirations unbidden and against my will" mentioned in a letter to Bridges for Sept. 1, 1885. It touches on some of the reasons for the feeling of desolation recorded in the "terrible" sonnets.

1   It seems to Hopkins that his lot in life is to appear —in spite of his longing for friendship—a stranger among strangers. This fate is all the more keenly borne in on him since his coming to Ireland.

2   Even while in England, he had been estranged from his dear parents, brothers and sisters, by his conversion to the Catholic Church and subsequent entrance into the Society of Jesus. In a letter to Newman for Oct. 15, 1866, he described their reaction to the news of his conversion as "terrible".

3   Though "dear" to him by natural consanguinity, he laments that they are "in Christ not near", as separated in religion.

4   Moreover, Christ himself, who is "prince of peace" (*Isaiah* ix. 6) and most sways his "spirits to peace" (*Duns Scotus's Oxford*), is yet for him an occasion of "strife" and separation. For so Christ warned his disciples:
      "Do not think that I came to bring peace upon earth; I came not to bring peace, but the sword. I came to set a man at variance against his father .... And a man's enemies shall be those of his own household." (*Matt.* x. 34–6)

5   He is cut off from his native country, England, not only as an exile in Ireland, but also as opposed to her Irish policy. Yet with all his heart he desires her true honour, which he "woos" in a kind of courtship. He acknowledges her as "wife to my creating thought", in that he derives his poetic inspiration from his homeland.

6 He complains that England would pay no attention to his plea, even if he pleaded like the "lovely dale" of *Ribblesdale*; since he has been unable to get any of his poems published there.

7 So he does not attempt to plead—though, as he declares in a letter of Mar. 2, 1885, to his mother:
   "The grief of mind I go through over politics, over what I read and hear and see in Ireland about England, is such that I can neither express it nor bear to speak of it." (FL 170)
   Like Hamlet, he must perforce keep silent: "But break, my heart, for I must hold my tongue!" (i. 2)

8 All he feels is weariness in remaining idle, peaking "like John-a-dreams, unpregnant of my cause" (*Hamlet* ii. 2), while around him "wars are rife". He is weighed down by "time's tasking" and "the sodden-with-its-sorrowing heart" (WD 27), which draws from him an echo of Hamlet's lament:
   "How weary, stale, flat and unprofitable
       Seem to me all the uses of this world." (i. 2)
   Here "but" has the meaning of "and yet": he is forced to remain idle, while those around him are at strife, a situation which makes him feel all the more frustrated.

9 He goes on to reflect how he is "in Ireland now" and thus "at a third remove" from home—the first remove having presumably been his conversion at Oxford, and the second his entrance into the Jesuit noviciate at Roehampton.

10 But even in exile from his family and his native country, he is not altogether deprived of comfort and "kind love"—where "kind" is used in the sense both of generous and of natural.

11 Moreover, this love is mutual, both given and received. He is, no doubt, thinking of his Jesuit confreres in Dublin, as well as his colleagues at University College.

12 Amid this "kind love", however, he finds himself unable
    give poetic expression to the thoughts that his heart
    "breeds" in wisdom. His every "heart-throe, birth of
    a brain" (WD 30), seems doomed to frustration, either
    by some "baffling ban" of God's inscrutable providence,
    or else by an evil "spell" cast by the powers of hell.
    "Ban" has the meaning of prohibition, with a possible
    suggestion of excommunication — exclusion from the
    company of heaven.

13 His thoughts, therefore, he must hoard like treasures
    within his heart, without uttering them in the hearing
    of others.

14 Or if he utters them, he finds they only pass unheeded.
    So in his frustration he feels like the man in Christ's
    parable (*Luke* xiv. 30) who "began" to build a tower,
    but was unable to finish it. "Began" is elliptical
    for "one who began,", as in the phrase "an also-ran"
    for one who ran in a race without success. Thus the
    poem itself ends where it "began", without having
    made any apparent progress.

25.

I wake and feel

I wake and feel

I WÁKE and féel the féll of dárk, not dáy.
What hóurs, O whát black hóürs wé have spént
This night! what síghts you, héart, saw; wáys you
    wént!
And móre must, ín yet lónger líght's deláy.

With wítness I spéak thís. But whére I sáy   5
Hóurs I mean yéars, mean lífe. And mý lamént
Is críes cóuntless, críes like dead létters sént
To déarest hím that líves alás! awáy.

I am gáll, I am héartburn. Gód's most déep decrée
Bítter would háve me táste: my táste was mé;   10
Bones búilt in mé, flesh fílled, blood brímmed the
    cúrse.

Selfyéast of spírit a dúll dough sóurs. I sée
The lóst are like thís, and théir scóurge to bé
As Í am míne, their swéating sélves; but wórse.

Commentary: The poem is undated, and is probably, like
the preceding, one of those mentioned in the letter of
Sept. 1, 1885. It is the darkest of the "terrible"
sonnets, beginning where *No worst* left off, and ending
as it were in the very depths of hell, with the addition,
"but worse".

1 Whereas the poet ended his sonnet *No worst* with the
comforting thought that at least the sorrows of each
day die "with sleep", he now finds himself deprived
even of this comfort, as he tosses in "fitful fever"
(*Macbeth* iii. 2) on his sleepless bed. "I wake" is
probably not "I wake up", but "I lie awake". All he
feels is the "fell", or cruel skin (combining both
meanings), of the dark, compared—as in WD 7 and
Carrion Comfort—to a devouring monster dandling
him in its terrible paws.

2 The hours of the night seem to have stood still,
leaving him to the full intensity of his anguish—like
the "anxious worried women" in Eliot's *Dry Salvages*,
who lie "awake, calculating the future. . . when time
stops and time is never ending". He emphasizes the
prolongation of time by marking a diaeresis over ü
in the second "hours". He speaks of himself in the
plural as "we", referring to himself and his heart, his
only companion in suffering, as in the later sonnet *My
own heart*.

3 Together, he and his heart have seen such sights,
travelled such ways, as are indescribable to those who
have not experienced the same.

4 Nor are they over yet; for the night is not yet done.
By "night" he means not just the material night that
ends with dawn, but the "dark night of the soul"
that only ends with the return of Christ as "a dayspring to the dimness of us" (WD 35). But he continually delays his coming (cf. *II. Peter* iii. 9).

5 This experience of desolation is not peculiar to his
own case, but is one to which all spiritual writers

bear "witness", such as St. John of the Cross in *The Dark Night of the Soul* and St. Ignatius in his *Rules for the Discernment of Spirits.*

6   It seems to him that he is condemned to continue in this state, not only for hours, but for years, and even for the rest of his life. For man's life on earth is, as Job remarks, "a warfare" (viii. 1), a state of separation from God, and thus of continual night in contrast with the eternal day of heavenly life.

7   His lament consists of "cries countless" sent up to God, who only turns a deaf ear on them. He compares them to "dead letters", appeals which remain unanswered, as if they were meaningless formalities.

8   In all this he feels no indignation against God, who remains his "dearest" (as he inscribes his letters to friends like Bridges). But he feels that God is far away and so fails to receive his letters.

9   He goes on, in the sestet, to generalize his present affliction in terms of his human sinfulness. He seems even to identify himself with the "gall" of bitterness, and with the "heartburn"—"the heartache and the thousand natural shocks that flesh is heir to"—of which Hamlet speaks in his famous soliloquy (iii. 1). He attributes all to God's decree, whose justice is to him, as to Job, quite incomprehensible. On this point, Hopkins changed "deep" to "just", but reverted to his original choice in the final version.

10   He is therefore filled with the taste of bitterness; or rather, he is himself that taste. As he says of the souls in hell in his spiritual notes:
     "*They*, their sins are the bitterness, tasted sweet once, now taste most bitter; no worm but themselves gnaws them and gnaws no one but themselves." (SD 243)

11   "The curse"—namely, "the blight man was born for" (*Spring and Fall*) on account of Adam's sin—seems to have grown up with him, even while God

"bound bones and veins in me, fastened me flesh" (WD 1). His bones, as it were, built it in him; his flesh filled it up; and his blood brimmed it "in a flash full" (WD 8).

12 Finally, the selfish spirit of man, like yeast, enters into the dough of his body and "sours" it "with sinning" ﹙*Spring*﹚, making it "dull" and heavy instead of light and airy. That "selfyeast" is here the subject of "sours", with "dull dough" as object, is clear from the variants in the first draft of the poem:

"Flesh fills, blood feeds/ this curse
Of my self stuff, by self yeast soured. I see
The lost are like this, with their loss/ to be
Their sweating selves, as I am mine, but worse."
"This curse—
Self stuff, and by selfyeast so soured
by yeasty self so soured."
"Selfyeast of spirit my selfstuff sours."

13 He even ventures to compare his state with that of the damned, or "lost" souls in hell.

14 He thinks of them, not as tormented by devils, as in the mediaeval imagination, but merely as left to themselves, their own worst "scourge"—"a rack where, selfwrung, selfstrung, sheathe- and shelterless, thoughts against thoughts in groans grind" (*Spelt from Sibyl's Leaves*). It is, he feels, the same with himself. The difference is merely one of degree: their pains he admits, as if by an afterthought, to be "worse" than his. This is the "dark side" of that theory of selfhood proposed so eloquently in the sonnet *As kingfishers*.

26.

Patience

Patience

PÁTIENCE, hárd thing! the hárd thing bút to práy,
But bíd for, Pátience ís! Pátience who ásks
Wants wár, wants wóunds; wéary his tímes, his
    tásks;
To dó withóut, take tósses, ánd obéy.

Rare pátience róots in thése, and, thése awáy,   5
Nówhere. Nátural heart's ívy, Pátience másks
Our rúins of wrécked past púrpose. Thére she básks
Purple éyes and séas of líquid léaves all dáy.

We héar our héarts gráte on themsélves: it kílls
To brúise them déarer. Yét the rebéllious wílls   10
Of ús we do bíd God bénd to him éven só.

And whére is hé who móre and móre distils
Delícious kíndness?—He is pátient. Pátience fílls
His crísp cómbs, and that cómes those wáys we
    knów.

Commentary: This poem is also undated, but is probably among those referred to in Hopkins' letter of Sept. 1, 1885. It also develops a theme in *King Lear*: "You heavens, give me that patience; patience I need!" (ii. 4)

1 The poet begins with general considerations on the virtue of patience. To him it seems a "hard thing", not only to acquire or to practise, but even to pray for.

2 "Bid" is here used in the original sense of pray, as in the German *bieten*; while also including the modern sense of offer money, as in *The Starlight Night*: "Buy then! bid then!"

3 He considers that one who asks for the gift of patience is equivalently asking for the conditions under which alone this gift has meaning: namely, "war" and the "wounds" that follow. He must be prepared for weariness in "his times, his tasks"—for "the jading and jar of the cart", which is "time's tasking" (WD 27).

4 He must learn to "do without" the comforts of life; to "take tosses"—submit to the reverses of fortune, like a rider who is thrown from his horse's back; and to "obey", as Albany says at the conclusion of *King Lear*: "The weight of this sad time we must obey" (v. 3).

5 It is in these situations that patience, like a "rare" plant, takes root; and "these away", it cannot exist. The same construction appears in *Richard II*, where Mowbray, speaking of "reputation", adds: "That away, men are but gilded loam or painted clay" (i. 1).

6 More precisely, he goes on to compare patience to ivy, the natural ivy of the human heart, which "masks" or disguises ruins.

7 Just as ivy grows round ancient ruins and gives them a romantic appearance, so patience hides our "ruins

of wrecked past purpose", the ambitions we cherished for ourselves in the past but have failed to fulfil, "what might have been" as opposed to "what has been" (cf. Eliot's *Burnt Norton* I).

8   The purple berries and luxuriant leaves of the ivy are further compared to eyes that are red with weeping, and tears like seas flowing from them. "Basks" is usually intransitive, but here it seems used in a transitive sense, with "eyes" and "seas" as object—unless perhaps these latter are in apposition to the subject: "She basks (with) purple eyes and seas. . . ."

9   From these general thoughts, the poet turns to himself and to God. In his troubles, he feels his heart "grate on" itself. So, too, he describes in *Spelt from Sibyl's Leaves* how "thoughts against thoughts in groans grind". In this self-torment there is something jarring and cacophonous which grates on his nerves, like an old oak door grating on its rusty hinges.

10 He feels that to inflict any "dearer" or deeper bruises on his heart would be tantamount to suicide. Yet he recalls the prayer of the Church's liturgy for the fourth Sunday after Pentecost: "Graciously compel even our rebellious wills to serve thee". Cf. WD 9: "Wring thy rebel, dogged in den, man's malice, with wrecking and storm."

11 In this prayer we ask God to bend our rebellious wills to his divine will, however much we may have to suffer in the process.

12 He goes on to ask: Well, where is he, after all? Where is he who increasingly distils the "delicious kindness" of his love, like a precious liqueur, through the sufferings of men?

13 At once he answers himself: God, too, is patient; and it is through his experience of patience that man learns to become like God.

14 It is patience, on both sides, which fills the honey-combs of God, namely the sources of his sweetness which from the outside seem so "crisp" and hard. And this comes to us "those ways we know" in deed, but cannot describe in word. Cf. WD 6: "And few know this"; and *Pied Beauty*: "Who knows how?" Thus the inscrutable decrees of "dark heaven" (*To seem the stranger*) begin to appear full of light and comfort, after all.

27.

My own heart

My own heart

MY ówn heart lét me móre have píty on; lét
Me líve to my sád sélf hereáfter kínd,
Cháritable; nót live thís torménted mínd
With thís torménted mínd torménting yét.

I cást for cómfort I can nó more gét   5
By gróping róund my cómfortléss, than blínd
Éyes in their dárk can dáy or thírst can fínd
Thirst's áll-in-áll in áll a wórld of wét.

Sóul, self; cóme, poor Jáckself, I dó advíse
You, jáded, lét be; cáll off thóughts awhíle   10
Élsewhere; leave cómfort róot-room; lét joy síze

At Gód knows whén to Gód knows whát; whose
     smíle
's not wrúng, see you; únforeséen times ráther—
     as skíes
Betwéenpie móuntains—líghts a lóvely míle.

Commentary: This poem is also undated, and is probably mentioned, with the preceding poems, in the letter for Sept. 1, 1885. It represents a further development from the previous sonnet, as the poet exhorts himself to desist from self-torment and to rest awhile.

1 He begins by urging himself to have more pity on his "own heart", as though multiplying himself into three—in the subject, the direct object, and the indirect object.

2 He urges himself to be more "kind" and "charitable" to his "sad self" than he has hitherto been.

3 He must not go on "tormenting yet" his sufficiently "tormented mind" by means of his "tormented mind". In these two lines he distinguishes various layers of self with almost as much subtlety as Duns Scotus, the Subtle Doctor: a) the self who is speaking; b) the self who is being spoken to; c) the self who is being tormented by b); d) the self whose torment is being used to inflict further torment on c).

5 He proceeds to describe his search for comfort, as in *No worst*: "Comforter, where, where is your comforting?" He casts his eyes round for a comfort he cannot find.

6 He compares his condition to that of a blind man "groping round" his room. Here "comfortless" is an adjective used as a noun ("state" or "condition" being understood), like "dark" in the following line.

7 He can no more find comfort in his comfortless condition, than "blind eyes" can find day "in their dark", or thirsty men on board ship can find water to drink in mid-ocean. His mention of blindness is no doubt suggested by the case of Milton, and so, too, of Samson in *Samson Agonistes*:
"O dark, dark, dark, amid the blaze of noon,
Irrecoverably dark, total eclipse
Without all hope of day!" (80–2)

8 His further mention of "thirst" likewise recalls
Coleridge's *Rime of the Ancient Mariner*: "Water,
water everywhere, nor any drop to drink". "All-in-
all" means of paramount importance, as used by St.
Paul in *I Corinthians*: "That God may be all in all"
(xv. 28). It is perhaps connected in the poet's mind
with Macbeth's "The be-all and the end-all" (i. 7).
The triple repetition of "all" reinforces the sense of
futility, as if emphasizing "not at all".

9 Such thoughts, however, only renew his self-torment;
and so he turns, in the sestet, to rebuke himself—as
on a different occasion in *The Candle Indoors*—with a
"Come, come!" He addresses himself as "poor Jackself", his common, workaday self, which need not be
made the object of such fuss. Similarly, he refers to
himself in *That Nature is a Heraclitean Fire* as "this
Jack, joke, poor potsherd".

10 All this self-torment only makes him "jaded", as with
"the jading and jar of the cart" (WD 27). He therefore exhorts himself to "let be"—leave things as they
are; to "call off" his thoughts, as a hunter might call
off his pack of hounds, and to direct them "elsewhere".

11 Only in this way will "comfort" have the necessary
room to send down and spread out its roots. So long
as he worries about himself, he does not give comfort
a chance! Here, as in the previous sonnet, he thinks
of comfort, as of patience, in terms of a plant—
"natural heart's ivy".

12 For "joy" will grow to the size that God only knows,
and in the time that God only knows. It is not for
him to determine "the times or the moments which
the Father has put in his own power" (*Acts* i. 7).

13 The "smile" or consolation of God is not to be
"wrung" or forced from him by the complaints of
any man. Rather, it is precisely when we are least

expecting it—"unforeseen times"—that his consolation
comes, like the Day of the Lord.

14 He compares it to the sunshine appearing unexpectedly
from behind dark clouds and lighting the road ahead
for "a lovely mile". More exactly, he thinks of a
landscape in which the "skies" are brilliantly dappled
between darker masses of mountains. Here "betweenpie" is the poet's own coinage, based on his favourite
epithet "pied", which he forms into a transitive verb
with the prefix "between". In this way, he rounds
off the series of "terrible" sonnets with a final vision
of comfort.

28.

St. Alphonsus Rodriguez

In honour of

St. Alphonsus Rodriguez

Laybrother of the Society of Jesus

HÓNOUR is flâshed off éxploit, só we sáy;
And thóse strokes ónce that gáshed flesh ór galled
shíeld
Should tóngue that tíme now, trúmpet nów that fíeld,
And, ón the fíghter, fórge his glórious dáy.
On Chríst they dó and ón the mártyr máy;   5
But bé the wár withín, the bránd we wíeld
Unséen, the heróic bréast not óutward-stéeled,
Earth héars no húrtle thén from fíercest fráy.
Yet Gód (that héws móuntain and cóntinént,
Earth, áll, out; whó, with tríckling incremént,   10
Veins víolets and táll trées makes móre and móre)
Could crówd caréer with cónquest whíle there wént
Those yéars and yéars by of wórld withóut evént
That ín Majórca Alfónso wátched the dóor.

Commentary: The first version of this poem dates from a letter to Bridges for Oct. 3, 1888, in which the poet writes:

> "I ask your opinion of a sonnet written to order on the occasion of the first feast since his canonisation proper of St. Alphonsus Rodriguez, a lay-brother of our Order, who for 40 years acted as hall-porter to the College of Palma in Majorca: he was, it is believed, much favoured by God with heavenly lights and much persecuted by evil spirits. The sonnet (I say it snorting) aims at being intelligible." (LB 292-3)

He comments on Bridges' criticism in a further letter for Oct. 19, which shows that he accepted some of his friend's amendments in his final version, while rejecting others (LB 296-7). The subject of the poem, St. Alphonsus Rodriguez ("Alfonso" in Spanish), lived from 1532 to 1617, and was canonized—that is, formally declared Saint by the Pope—on Sept. 6, 1887. His annual feast is kept on Oct. 31.

1 The poet begins by speaking in a general way of the "honour" or reputation that is won by great deeds on the field of battle. It is "flashed off" them, as it were a glimpse of God's own grandeur. The line originally read: "Honour should flash from exploit", and was subsequently changed to: "Glory is a flame off exploit", before reaching its final form. In his reply to Bridges, Hopkins insists on his use of the word "exploit", as being "the right word" and "a handsome word" at that. He also justifies the addition "so we say", as being "just what I have to say and want to say", with the meaning: "This is what we commonly say, but we are wrong" (LB 297).

2 He then refers to the battle-field, on which the flesh of the fighter is "gashed" and his shield "galled" by the sword-strokes of the enemy. Beyond the enemy, he looks implicitly to "the stroke dealt" by God (WD 6), and to the providence by which "blue-bleak embers

...fall, gall themselves, and gash gold-vermilion"
The Windhover).

3 The scars of these strokes that remain on flesh and
shield give eloquent "tongue" now to those deeds of
the past, and serve as a lasting "trumpet" of that
battlefield.

4 At the time they were dealt, "with an anvil-ding"
(WD 10), they forged "on the fighter" his glory for
days to come.

5 The poet next turns to the thought of Christ and his
saints, as fighters in a spiritual warfare. He reflects
how Christ, too, bears the marks of combat in the
five wounds of his hands, feet and side, his "cinque-
foil token"; and how "he scores it in scarlet himself
on his own bespoken" (WD 22)—openly, in the case
of those martyrs who were physically wounded and
put to death.

6 But in most cases, the spiritual warfare is "within",
as in Christ's temptation by Satan in the desert; and
there "the brand we wield" has to be the "sword of
the spirit", of which St. Paul speaks in *Ephesians*
vi. 17.

7 Similarly, the breastplate protecting the spiritual hero
is one not of outward steel, but of inward "justice",
as St. Paul says in the same place (vi. 14).

8 In such cases, the event, heroic though it be, passes
unnoticed on earth. The "fray", however fierce,
makes no hurtling or clashing sound—like "the hurtle
of hell" (WD 3)—to attract the attention of other
men.

9 After these general considerations, the poet comes to
the theme of his poem, in an impressive sentence
that moves from the creative action of God to the
humble work of Alfonso as hall-porter. He presents
God, in the manner of St. Ignatius' Contemplation
for Obtaining Love, as a workman "that hews" by

the power of his word mountain—"his world-wielding shoulder" (*Hurrahing in Harvest*)—continent and earth, in progressively expanding order. This idea is even more strongly expressed in the first version, which speaks of God as "the mountain-mason, continent-quarrier, earthwright". He also used the verb "builds" before hitting on "hews". The latter word he justifies in his letter of Oct. 19:

"Whatever is markedly featured in stone or what is like stone is most naturally said to be hewn, and to *shape*, itself, means in old English to hew and the Hebrew *bara* / to create, even, properly means to hew." (LB 296–7)

10 Whereas God acts with might and mastery upon brute matter, forging his will there "with an anvil-ding", he acts upon living things "with a lingering-out sweet skill" (WD 10), through the "trickling increment" of sap which is drawn up drop by drop from the roots of the plant. On this process Hopkins continues in the above letter:

"But life and living things are not naturally said to be hewn: they grow, and their growth is by trickling increment." (LB 297)

11 By this gradual osmosis, he "veins violets" symbols of humility, with their delicate shades of colour, and, on the other hand, gives daily increase to "tall trees"—attending no less to the lowly than to the lofty.

12 It is also he who, on the human level, crowds "career with conquest"—whether the material conquests of the Spanish "conquistadores" in the New World during Alfonso's lifetime, or the less spectacular but none the less momentous spiritual conquests of Alfonso himself.

13 In contrast to the events of the outside world during the Golden Age of Spain, the life of Alfonso seemed to pass by year after year "without event". Perhaps this was the "witness" to which the poet appealed in

his sonnet *I wake*: "But where I say hours I mean years, mean life."

14 The climax to the poem is simplicity itself, corresponding to the simplicity with which "in Majorca Alfonso watched the door". Yet now he has received the supreme "honour" of canonization from the Church he served so faithfully.

29.

Thou art indeed just

Thou art indeed just

Justus quidem tu es, Domine, si disputem tecum:
verumtamen justa loquar ad te: Quare via impiorum
prosperatur? &c.

THOU árt indéed júst, Lord, if Í conténd
With thée; bút, sir, so whát I pléad is júst.
Whý do sínners' ways prósper? and whý múst
Dísappóintment áll I endéavour énd?

Wért thou my énemy, Ó thóu my fríend,   5
Hów wouldst thou wórse, I wónder, thán thou dóst
Deféat, thwárt me? Oh, the sóts and thrálls of lúst
Dó in spare hóurs more thríve than Í that spénd,

Sir, lífe upón thy cáuse. See, bánks and brákes
Now, léavèd how thíck! lácèd they áre agáin   10
With frétty chérvil, lóok, and frésh wind shákes

Them; bírds búild—but not Í build; nó, but stráin,
Time's éunuch, ánd not bréed one wórk that wákes.
Míne, O thou lórd of lífe, send mý roots ráin.

Commentary: The poem is dated "March 17, '89". In place of a title, it bears a text from the Latin Vulgate, *Jeremiah* xii. 1, which may be literally translated:

"Thou art indeed just, Lord, if I dispute with thee; yet what I say to thee is just: Why does the way of the impious prosper?"

In a letter to Bridges, for March 20, 1889, Hopkins says of this sonnet that "it must be read *adagio molto* and with great stress."

1 The poet opens with an almost literal translation of the text which serves as his title. The theme is one that is deep in the Old Testament "wisdom" literature: not only in *Jeremiah*, but also in *Job* ix and xxi, in *Ecclesiastes* viii. 14, and in *Psalms* xlix and lxxiii.

2 He addresses God as "sir", somewhat as a pupil might address his master. Perhaps he is thinking, like Milton in the sonnet *On His Blindness*, of God as "task-master", or "martyr-master" (WD 21). "So" may have the sense of provided that; but it more probably follows on "plead", in the sense of thus, by way of contention.

3 On the one hand, it seems—as Jeremiah, Job and Ecclesiastes point out in the above-mentioned passages —that the ways of sinners are prosperous.

4 On the other hand, it seems that everything he tries to do, whether in his priestly ministry or in poetic composition, only ends in disappointment and failure. As he laments in *To seem the stranger*, he feels "a lonely began".

5 On the basis of this Scriptural text, he proceeds to complain, in the daring language of saints like St. Teresa of Avila, that God seems to be rather his enemy than his friend—though, as in the "terrible" sonnet *I wake*, he clings to his faith in God's love.

6 After all, if God were his enemy, he could hardly do more to defeat and thwart him than he actually does. Perhaps it is the alliteration with "w" which

makes the poet replace the normal construction "wouldst thou do more to defeat" with "wouldst worse defeat".

7 He contrasts his own frustration with the flourishing condition of "the sots and thralls of lust"—those who are befooled and enslaved by the lusts of the flesh.

8 Even in their "spare" moments they "thrive" more than he does who spends his whole life in the service of God.

9 Once again he addresses God somewhat formally as "sir". After "spend" one would expect the preposition "in"; but the alternative "upon" seems to be inserted here for the rhythm. The sestet is not clearly distinguished in this sonnet. If anywhere, it begins half-way through the line, with the change of tone introduced by the reference to natural scenery. Here he momentarily looks up from his sorrows to take notice of the "banks and brakes", the hedgerows and thickets of the countryside which are already showing the new green of spring. The phrase is reminiscent of Burns' song, "Ye banks and braes o' bonny Doon".

10 Already in the middle of March he finds them thick with leaves, and once more "laced" or intertwined with "chervil", a wild plant related to parsley, whose leaves are characterized as "fretty" or finely indented.

11 He further stimulates his attention with a "look!", noticing how these plants are shaken by the "fresh wind", the cold east wind that blows over England during March. Here he perhaps echoes Shakespeare's *Sonnet* xviii: "Rough winds do shake the darling buds of May".

12 He thinks of the birds building their nests in the trees and hedges, in a development of thought similar to that in *Spring*; but again he cannot help reflecting on the contrast with his own condition: "Birds build

—but not I build", with an echo of Milton's lament in *Paradise Lost* III 40–2:

> "Thus with the year
> Seasons return, but not to me returns
> Day, or the sweet approach of ev'n or morn."

13 All he can do is to "strain", making fruitless endeavours at poetic composition, without apparently being able to produce "one work that wakes"—one poem that lives and lasts to posterity. He feels himself as it were "Time's eunuch", in contrast those "who have made themselves eunuchs for the kingdom of heaven" (*Matt.* xix. 12). As priest and religious, he belongs to the latter class; but as poet, he seems to belong to the former.

14 He concludes, however, not on this pessimistic note, but with a prayer to God as "lord of life" to send rain on the dry roots of his poetic inspiration. The opening word "Mine" (the old form of "my" before a vowel) may modify "lord" or "life" or even "roots" (reinforcing the other "my"). The title "lord of life" is derived from *Acts* iii, 15, and echoes WD 1: "Lord of living and dead"—where he found the hand of God touching him afresh and exclaimed: "Over again I feel thy finger and find thee". The image of "roots" is here significantly repeated from two of the "terrible" sonnets: *Patience*: "Rare patience roots in these", and *My own heart*: "Leave comfort root-room". Here he has the roots, but not the rain for their nourishment.

30.

The shepherd's brow

The shepherd's brow

The shépherd's brów, frónting forked líghtning, ówns
The hórror ánd the hávoc ánd the glóry
Of it. Ángels fáll, they are tówers, from héaven—a
    stóry
Of júst, majésticál and gíant gróans.
But mán—we, scáffold of scóre bríttle bónes;   5
Who bréathe, from gróundlong bábyhóod to hóary
Age gásp; whose bréath is oúr *meménto móri*—
What báss is *óur* víol for trágic tónes?
He! Hánd to móuth he líves, and vóids with sháme;
And, blázoned ín howéver bóld the náme,   10
Man Jáck the mán is, júst; his máte a hússy.
And Í that díe these déaths, that féed this fláme,
That. . . ín smooth spóons spy lífe's masque mír-
    rored: táme
My témpests thére, my fíre and féver fússy.

Commentary: The final draft of the poem is dated "April 3, 1889", being the outcome of four previous drafts. It was relegated by Bridges to the end of the "Unfinished Poems, Fragments" in his first edition, on the grounds that it "must have been thrown off one day in a cynical mood". His decision was accepted by W. H. Gardner in the third edition, where he quotes Hopkins' remark to Bridges: "A cynical vein much indulged coarsens everything in us" (LB 148). The poem is, however, restored to its rightful place among the poems in the fourth edition, on the grounds that Hopkins took it sufficiently seriously to write five drafts of it. Nor is it necessarily cynical: it represents the same realistic approach to man's mortality as in WD 11: "But we dream we are rooted in earth—Dust!" It has been compared with Hamlet's "Man delights not me!" (ii. 2)

1 The poet begins by citing two examples of heroic events, to set in contrast to ordinary human beings like himself. His thoughts go back to Moses, "that shepherd who first taught the chosen seed" (*Paradise Lost* I 8), who confronted the thunder and lightning on Mount Sinai in his meeting with God, with the result that "his face was horned from the conversation of the Lord" (*Exod.* xxxiv. 29). "Owns" is here used, as in *To what serves Mortal Beauty?*, in the double sense of "possesses" and "recognizes".

2 In the presence of God, man experiences "a horror of height" (WD 2), "strokes of havoc" that "unselve" (*Binsey Poplars*), and the "glory" of "thunder" (WD 5). Here the poet emphasizes rather the "lightning" than the "love" of God (WD 9).

3 For his second example, he follows the thought of Milton from Moses to the Fall of the Angels, which is described not in the books of Moses, but in the prophecy of Isaiah (xiv. 4–15). Cf. *Is.* xiv. 12: "How art thou fallen from heaven, O Lucifer!"; also the words of Christ in *Luke* x. 18: "I saw Satan like lightning falling from heaven". He is evidently

thinking of Milton's description of Satan in *Paradise Lost* I 589-91: "He above the rest/ In shape and gesture proudly eminent/ Stood like a tower"; and perhaps of the other fallen angel, Mulciber, who is said to have "built in heaven high towers" (I 749).

4 The "groans" of the fallen angels, as described in *Paradise Lost* I, are "just"—in the sense that they justly deserved punishment for having "durst defy the Omnipotent to arms" (I 49); "majestical"—in that their "form had not yet lost/ All her original brightness, nor appeared/ Less than archangel ruined" (I 591-3); and "giant"—in comparison with those "whom the fables name of monstrous size/ Titanian, or earth-born, that warred on Jove" (I 197-8).

5 The poet then rounds on man: "But man—", with the same feeling of "pity and indignation" as he shows in *That Nature is a Heraclitean Fire*, together with the further sense of disgust that appears in WD 11: "But we dream..." He thinks of man as a "scaffold" of bones, the "bone-house" of *The Caged Skylark*, with an echo of WD 1: "Thou hast bound bones and veins in me" (cf. *Job* x. 11). There is also an implication of the scaffold or stage of this world, on which each man must play his part; and of the scaffold on which man must ultimately meet Death, his executioner. "Brittle" emphasizes the frailty of mortal life; "score", its insignificance and brief duration (cf. Ps. cx. 10).

6 Our life on earth, while we "draw our breath in pain" (*Hamlet* v. 2), lasts from "groundlong babyhood"—crawling along the ground—to the final "gasp" of "hoary age", the white hairs of old men.

7 Our very breath, so shortly to be spent in death, serves to remind us of our end, like the skulls that used in former time to be kept for this purpose, with the inscription: "Memento mori" (Remember thou art to die).

8 Referring to Elizabethan musical instruments, he asks what "bass-viol" gives forth a deep enough sound to suit our "tragic tones". Here "bass" is short for "bass-viol" (ancestor of the 'cello), while "viol" is used in the generic sense.

9 For the next three lines he changes from the first person plural to the third person singular: from "we" to "he"—by way of preparing a contrast with the concluding "I". He concentrates on the purely vegetative side of human life: on the one hand, living from "hand to mouth" as he feeds, and, on the other, voiding "with shame" as he excretes waste matter.

10 His "name" or reputation may be "blazoned" to the world in bold characters,

11 yet he remains a mere "Jack", like "every man jack". Here Jack is used as a term of contempt, as so often in Shakespeare: cf. the amusing assertion of Falstaff in *1 Henry IV* v. 4: "If I be not Jack Falstaff, then am I a Jack". Hopkins likewise speaks of his "Jackself" in *My own heart*, and of "This Jack, joke, poor potsherd" in *That Nature is a Heraclitean Fire.* "Just" means precisely, exactly. In similar fashion, "his mate" is called "hussy" (from "housewife") in a somewhat contemptuous tone.

12 He finally turns to himself, drawing a further contrast between his tendency to dramatize his own sorrows and the fact of his insignificance. He tends to think of himself as dying "these deaths", whereas they are only "feigned deaths", as in Donne's *Song*; or else as feeding this living "flame"—whether the flame of suffering or the flame of love (cf. WD 3: "To flash from the flame to the flame").

13 There follows an anti-climax, marked by the dots after "That...", as he sees "life's poor play" (Pope, *Essay on Man* II) reflected and distorted in the concave mirror of "smooth spoons", which are such ordinary

utensils of daily life. Cf. T. S. Eliot's *Prufrock*: "I have measured out my life with coffee spoons".

14   This rather humiliating consideration serves to "tame" his stormy feelings, by making them seem mere "tempests in a tea-cup", and to abate the "fitful fever" of his life (*Macbeth* iii. 2). In this light he sees that he has been making a fuss about nothing. Such a conclusion, so far from being cynical, is in keeping with the *Spiritual Exercises* of St. Ignatius, who advises the retreatant in the Second Exercise of First Week to demean himself by various examples.

31.

To R.B.

To R.B.

THE fíne delíght that fáthers thóught; the stróng
Spur, líve and láncing líke the blówpipe fláme,
Breathes ónce and, quénchèd fáster thán it cáme,
Leaves yét the mínd a móther of immórtal sóng.

Nine mónths she thén, nay yéars, nine yéars she lóng   5
Withín her wéars, bears, cáres and cómbs the sáme:
The wídow of an ínsight lóst she líves, with aím
Now knówn and hánd at wórk now néver wróng.

Sweet fíre the síre of múse, my sóul needs thís;
I wánt the óne rápture of an ínspirátion.   10
O thén if ín my lágging línes you míss

The róll, the ríse, the cárol, thé creátion,
My wínter wórld, that scárcely bréathes that blíss
Now, yíelds you, with some síghs, our éxplanátion.

Commentary: The poem is dated "April 22, '89", and is dedicated in the title to his friend, Robert Bridges. It was sent to Bridges as "a new sonnet" in a letter for April 29, 1889.

1 The poet devotes the first four lines to a description of poetic inspiration in terms of marriage and conception of offspring. Such inspiration is a "fine delight" which begets poetic thought, as a father begets children.

2 It is a "strong spur" or impulse, charged with life, and a pointed or "lancing" movement like the flame from a "blowpipe".

3 It is akin to the "arch and original Breath" (WD 25) which breathed over the waters in creation; but, having performed its function, it is "quenched faster than it came"—just as man, the "clearest-selved spark of nature" is quenched in death (*That Nature is a Heraclitean Fire*).

4 Its effect is to make the mind "a mother of immortal song"—of a poetic masterpiece.

5 Pursuing the same metaphor, the poet now turns to the mind as mother, as she carries the thought within her womb for the nine months of gestation—or it may be, in fact, nine years, as he says in *I wake*, "but where I say hours, I mean years".

6 During all this time she bears the thought within her as a slowly forming child, looks after it and metaphorically combs its hair ever so gently. "Combs" was disapproved of by Bridges, who substituted "moulds" in its first publication; but "moulds" hardly fits into the alliterative movement of the line.

7 The mind is meanwhile "the widow of an insight" she has lost, as it was only momentary; but she continues to live, with a clear aim before her to be realized in the course of time.

8 The hand likewise, having this clear aim, is "now never wrong" in carrying it out.

9 All this is on a general level; but in the sestet the poet reflects on his own case, how this is precisely what his soul needs—that "sweet fire" which is the "sire" or father of poetry.

10 All he needs is "the one rapture of an inspiration" to make his mind "a mother of immortal song".

11 But he feels—and expects his friend to feel—that his lines are too heavy and "lagging behind", like an unwilling dog on a lead.

12 They lack that vitality of lyric impulse which is characteristic of a new creation—"a strain of the earth's sweet being in the beginning" (*Spring*).

13 His mental world is one, not of spring or summer, but of winter, "blue-bleak" (*The Windhover*) with scarcely a breath of the "heaven of desire" (WD 26).

14 All he can present, therefore, to his friend is this poetic explanation of his lack of poetic inspiration— "some sighs" in place of the one "breath" he longs for.

Appendix

Appendix: The Underthought of Shakespeare

In a letter for Jan. 14, 1883, to his friend, Alexander
Baillie, speaking of "any lyric passage of the tragic poets",
Hopkins distinguishes "two strains of thought running
together and like counterpointed".   One is "the overthought, that which everybody, editors see".   The other is
  "the underthought, conveyed chiefly in the choice of
  metaphors etc used and often only half realised by the
  poet himself, not necessarily having any connection with
  the subject in hand but usually having a connection and
  suggested by some circumstance of the scene or of the
  story."   (FL 252)
After discussing an example from Aeschylus' *Suppliants*
he adds:
  "Perhaps what I ought to say is that the underthought
  is commonly an echo or shadow of the overthought,
  something like canons and repetitions in music, treated
  in a different manner, but that sometimes it may be
  independent of it."   (FL 253)
This theory may well be applied to the imagery of
Hopkins' own sonnets, in which certain favourite ideas
and images reappear again and again — as the foregoing
commentary makes abundantly clear.   It may also be
applied to the various literary influences in the sonnets,
especially those of Shakespeare and Milton.   The influence
of the latter's *Paradise Lost* Book I, for example, is particularly evident in *The shepherd's brow*; and even more
pervasive is the "underthought" of Shakespeare's *King
Lear* in *No worst*—as I have shown at length in an article
on "The Underthought of Shakespeare in Hopkins", in
Studies in English Literature (Tokyo), March 1963.
Hopkins' admiration for Shakespeare, in particular,
forms a common theme in his correspondence with his

literary friends   To Richard Dixon he points out the peculiar beauty and effectiveness of the Shakespearian sonnet. To Robert Bridges he justifies his own theory of poetic language—that it should be "the current language heightened and unlike itself, but not an obsolete one"— by appealing to Shakespeare's practice (LB 89). Again, to Dixon he confesses that what attracts him in Shakespeare is "the breadth of his human nature" (LD 74), to which he later adds "the finest faculty of observation of all men that ever breathed" (LD 140). Finally, the abundance of his allusions and quotations from the plays of Shakespeare shows how deep was the influence on his thought and imagination of this "greatest of poets" (FL 219).

In the foregoing commentary many scattered references have been given to various passages in the poems and plays of Shakespeare. It may, therefore, be convenient to gather them together here in the form of a special appendix, in place of a general index which is unnecessary in a book of this kind. It will be noticed that most of the references are to the "great" tragedies, and that they most frequently occur in the later poems of the Dublin period. This points to an interesting correlation between Shakespeare's tragedies and Hopkins' "dark" sonnets, as a literary phenomenon of some importance.

*   *   *   *   *

As You Like It   56
Hamlet   61, 81, 99, 109, 129, 141, 143, 150, 154,
        189, 190
Henry IV Part I   191
Henry V   35, 93
Henry VIII   98
King John   77
King Lear   109, 147, 165
Love's Labour's Lost   76
Macbeth   6, 32, 109, 123, 143, 159, 172
Merchant of Venice   85, 110
Othello   87, 93-94, 122